Language, Literature, and the Dynamics of Conflict

CONTRIBUTORS

Eunice Ngongkum holds a PhD in African Literature from the University of Yaounde 1 where she is presently a Professor of African literature and culture in the Department of African Literature and Civilisations. Her research interests are in the domains of postcolonial African literature, Postcolonial ecocritical culture, Diaspora African literature, cultural studies, literary theory, and criticism. She has published widely on these subjects in peer-reviewed journals worldwide. Her monographs include *Anglophone Cameroon Poetry in the Environmental Matrix* (2017) and *Dennis Brutus' Poetics of Revolt* (2018). She has two collections of short stories and a volume of poetry to her credit.

Kelvin Ngong Toh is Associate Professor of African Literature and Cultures. He holds a PhD in African Literature and Civilisations from the University of Yaounde 1, Cameroon. He currently teaches African Literature and Cultures in the Department of English and Cultural Studies at the University of Buea and Postcolonial Literatures and Cultures at the University of Bamenda, where he also handles some administrative duties. He has published extensively in the area of migration, the ambivalence of borders in the global age and discussions on colonialism in Africa. His areas of research interest include African and African diaspora literatures and cultures, literary theory, film and music studies and postcolonialisms.

Mbuh Tennu Mbuh is an Associate Professor of British English in the Department of English at the University of Bamenda, Cameroon. He is a Fulbright and Commonwealth Scholar. He is currently serving as the Chair of the Department of English. His research interests include Post-independence Literature, Postcolonial Literature and Cameroon Literature. He has several publications in national and international peer-reviewed journals as well as many book chapters. He has co-edited numerous scientific research proceedings. He is the author of several artistic works, collections of poems, novels, and plays.

Ernest L. Veyu has a PhD from the University of Yaounde 1, Cameroon. He specialises in, and teaches British Literature, alongside Postcolonial Studies as a minor, in the same university. He has published several articles in national and international journals in these domains and is actively involved in research in his institution and beyond. He is the author of Virginia Woolf's Artists in

To the Lighthouse, The Making of the Modern Artist: Stephen Dedalus and Will Brangwen, Faultlines in Postcoloniality: Contemporary Readings, Globalisation and Transitional Ideologies: Moving the Margins through Language and Literature, edited with Stephen Mforteh, and ten collections of poems.

Nyanchi Marcel Ebliylu holds a PhD in Commonwealth Literature from the Department of English, University of Yaounde 1. He is senior lecturer of Postcolonial literatures and cultures in the Department of Applied Foreign Languages, University of Dschang. He has published articles in book chapters and peer-reviewed journals nationally and internationally. His research interests include Postcolonial studies, cultural studies, Gender studies and Critical theory.

Hans Mbonwuh Fonka is a lecturer in the Department of English at the University of Bamenda, Cameroon, where he also serves as coordinator of English Language. He is an Editorial Advisory Group member of Applied Linguistics for Cambridge Scholars Publishing. His research interest focuses on Contact Languages, especially Pidgins and Creoles, Language Learning, Language and Communication, phonetics and phonology, Varieties of English and Applied Linguistics. His research works have been published as book chapters and Journal articles both nationally and internationally.

Terence Nsai Kiwoh holds a PhD in Sociolinguistics from the University of Yaounde 1, and he is interested in issues of Identity, language policy and peace-building. He currently lectures at the University of Buea, Cameroon. He is the author of several publications in national and international peer-reviewed journals, as well as many book chapters.

Joseph Nkwain holds a PhD in English Linguistics from the University of Yaounde 1, Cameroon. He is currently a Senior Lecturer in the Department of Bilingual Letters at the University of Maroua where he teaches aspects of English/French Comparative/Contrastive Studies, Translation Studies, English Usage, English Grammar and Lexicology. His research interests include the New Englishes, Internet Linguistics, Postcolonial Pragmatics, Sociolinguistics and Discourse Analysis. He has several publications in national and international peer-reviewed journals as well as many book chapters to his credit.

LANGUAGE, LITERATURE, AND THE DYNAMICS OF CONFLICT

Edited by
Eunice Ngongkum
Hans Mbonwuh Fonka

SPEARS BOOKS
DENVER, COLORADO

Spears Books
An Imprint of Spears Media Press LLC
7830 W. Alameda Ave, Suite 103-247
Denver, CO 80226
United States of America

First Published in the United States of America in 2023 by Spears Books
www.spearsbooks.org
info@spearsbooks.org
@spearsbooks

Information on this title: www.spearsbooks.org/language-literature-and-the-dynamics-of-conflict/

© 2023 Eunice Ngongkum & Hans M. Fonka
All rights reserved.

No part of this publication may be reproduced, distributed, or transmitted in any form or by any means, including photocopying, recording, or other electronic or mechanical methods, without the prior written permission of the publisher, except in the case of brief quotations embodied in critical reviews and certain other noncommercial uses permitted by copyright law. For permission requests, write to the publisher, addressed "Attention: Permissions Coordinator," at the above address.

ISBN: 9781957296241 (Paperback)
ISBN: 9781957296258 (eBook)

Spears Media Press has no responsibility for the persistence or accuracy of urls for external or third-party internet websites referred to in this publication, and does not guarantee that any content on such websites is, or will remain, accurate or appropriate.

Designed and typeset by Spears Media Press LLC
Cover designed by D. Kambem

Distributed globally by African Books Collective (ABC)
www.africanbookscollective.com

To all Frontier Research Group members

Contents

Acknowledgments — xiii
Introduction — xv
List of Abbreviations — xx

PART ONE: LITERARY INTERROGATIONS OF CONFLICT

1. "The Agony of my Country": Sierra Leone's Turbulent History in Syl Cheney-Coker's Poetry — 1
   Eunice Ngongkum

2. Bob Marley and the Discourse of Conflict — 16
   Kelvin Ngong Toh

3. Spatial Transcendence and the (Re)Invention of Space in James Joyce's *A Portrait of the Artist as a Young Man* — 30
   Mbuh Tennu Mbuh

4. Male Assertion and the Arts in Virginia Woolf's *To the Lighthouse* — 51
   Ernest L. Veyu

5. Re-Building Paradise: Islamic Ecosphere in Salman Rushdie's *The Satanic Verses* — 67
   Marcel Ebliylu Nyanchi

PART TWO: LANGUAGE, CONFLICT CREATION AND CONFLICT RESOLUTION

6. Insults and Spear Words in Music: Cameroon Pidgincreole as a Battle Shield   87
   Hans Mbonwuh Fonka

7. Mitigating Linguistic Identity differences in Cameroon: The Role of Bilingual Education   109
   Kiwoh Terence Nsai

8. The Power of Language in Persuasion: A Lexico-semiotic Reading of Evangelisation Crusade Posters in Cameroon   124
   Joseph Nkwain

Index   143

TABLES

Table 6.1 Creations in Pidgin	92
Table 6.2 Unfamiliar Lexical items	102
Table 6.3 Lexical adaptation	103
Table 7.1 Frequency and Time Distribution per Subject in HOBEC Douala 3e B or Four B	118

FIGURES

Figure 6.1 Data points	98
Figure 6.2 Data point differential view	99
Figure 6.3 Same data point differential view from another angle	99
Figure 8.1 The Persuasion Model developed by Feldman (1994)	128

Acknowledgments

The editors of *Language, Literature and the Dynamics of Conflict* are thankful to Frontiers Research Group for organising the conference during which the papers in this book were presented. We express our gratitude to all Frontier Members who took part during that conference and provided inputs which have shaped the different chapters in this book. We are particularly indebted to our reviewers for taking off time to review these papers. Their insightful comments helped the authors to have a re-examination of their papers.

INTRODUCTION

The current resurgence of conflicts on a global scale invites a re-visioning of crucial parameters on which human society is constructed, namely, identity, borders, natural resources, religion, cultural values/beliefs, governance, ideology, globalisation, and other social relationships, among others. The Middle East, Africa, Asia, South America, and Europe are witnessing conflicts that touch on one or more factors. LeBaron (2003) notes that "Conflict, put simply, is a difference that matters." These perceived differences that matter, broadly speaking, intersect the cultural, ethnic, religious, and political. The escalating costs of conflicts at these different levels have, concomitantly, increased the need for resolution or prevention, as the case may be. The practical nature of conflict resolution/prevention, including a commitment to responsiveness and critical personal engagement on the part of conflict resolution scholars and practitioners, is an important resource for working across difference in the world today. Three or four decades ago, avoidance, or the threat of force or court action as the choice for managing disputes would likely have been the first and possibly only conflict prevention/resolution method. In contemporary society, mediation and other well-known conflict prevention/resolution processes are now valued and accepted as real options for addressing various conflicts. The resulting encounters across differences are foregrounded through everyday life in complex and unexpected ways which speak to key contemporary political, religious, and economic challenges in the global sphere. In this framework, the arts, in general, play a crucial but somewhat under-explored role. They often provide unusual and complex perspectives on conflict situations prone to oversimplification and play a key role in helping people come to terms with a legacy of violence, thereby contributing to peace building.

This collection of original essays seeks to assess the role of language and literature in creating, preventing, and resolving conflicts in contemporary contexts. Through a variety of lenses, the papers interrogate various perspectives of conflict, bringing to light an interesting vision of how language and literature have attended to this perennial issue.

PART ONE: LITERARY INTERROGATIONS OF CONFLICT

The very essence of literature, it has been acknowledged, is sustained by paradigms of conflict at the individual, social, political, and cultural levels. How individuals and communities respond to such tensions makes interesting reading, as the essays here reveal.

Eunice Ngongkum's "The Agony of my Country": Sierra Leone's Turbulent History in Syl Cheney-Coker's Poetry," examines the 1991 war in Sierra Leone from the perspective of one of the country's foremost poets, Syl Cheney-Coker. From a New Historicist perspective, the essay argues that in the poetry, the seeds of the persistent conflict and eventual war in the country lie beyond the country's diamonds, even though problems in the diamond sector did indeed contribute to the war (See Boas 2001, Keen 2003, Reno 2003 & Wigglesworth 2008). The poetry indicates that the conflict-laden history and politics of the postcolony inexorably led the country into violent civil strife. While this may sound clichéd for those conversant with Sierra Leonean history, the chapter argues that the way in which the genre of poetry recreates and exposes the horrors that precipitated Sierra Leone into civil war makes interesting reading. Through a visionary and cautionary aesthetics, Cheney-Coker explores the historical antecedents of Sierra Leone's gradual decline into anarchy and civil war. Ngongkum's overall argument hinges on the fact that in a time of crisis, the poetic genre is multifaceted enough for "making a statement, for bearing witness, for instigating a humane social and moral order and for conscientizing the reader to a better understanding of the corruption of power and the patent often brazen, nature of evil" (Achebe, quoted in Obiechina, p. 529).

From the popular cultural perspective, Kelvin Ngong Toh discusses Bob Marley's songs as compositions that the artist uses to reveal conflicts. For him, what Marley does in his music is in line with the intellectual argument that art should be on the side of the oppressed against their oppressors, as propounded by theorists like Ngugi wa Thiong'o (1982) and Edward Said (1996). For the latter, commitment occurs in such contexts when the artist and/or intellectual takes the side of the "people." While this perspective might be limiting, especially when dealing with political or committed art, the chapter argues that Marley's music subscribes to this kind of logic. This position, the essay states, is very relevant in this reading of Marley's songs because there is a socio-cultural root to all conflicts that betray such ambiguities.

In the chapter entitled "Spatial Transcendence" and the (Re) Invention of Space in James Joyce's *A Portrait of the Artist as a Young Man*," Mbuh Tennu Mbuh notes that modernism and its scrutiny of traditional borderlines while opting for more impalpable zones of existence, was the outcome of the "traditional" world becoming a contested site in the wake of new intellectual and artistic insights in the imagination of the West. The collapse of the Empire with the ensuing Commonwealth of Nations grappling anew for universal conquest was challenged by the United Kingdom's closest neighbour, staying out of the bloc. The fact that one of the greatest writers of the twentieth century, James Joyce, hailed from Ireland and struggled in both his life and writing to reconcile with his Anglo-Irish identity proves the delicate nature of colonial boundary formations and their implications. In discussing the notion of borders and the spaces they demarcate in Joyce's *A Portrait*, this chapter argues that the novel imagines new spaces by overriding previous linear or binary constructs and replaces them with concentric variants from the bolting imagination of the hero. At the same time, it is apparent that in creating a hero who seeks newer frontiers with only a vague hope and promise to return, Joyce sacrificed the physical space of nationalist passions for the virtual alternative of the escapist exile. This ambivalence makes *A Portrait* counter-productive to the nationalist agenda of ascertaining space and borders and ironically enhances the neutralisation of borders, which colonialism nurtured.

In Ernest L. Veyu's "Male Assertion and the Arts in Virginia Woolf's *To the Lighthouse*," the conflict between male and female relations to the subject of art is laid bare. The chapter argues that art is worsted in the fight for male superiority and in the pursuit of female emancipation. The patriarchal assumption that art is for men automatically excludes women. In such a context, Virginia Woolf's portrait of the men shows them as chauvinistic, insensitive, assertive, clumsy, ugly, violent, sterile, venerable, syllogistic, etc. On the other hand, the women are generous, caring, loving, tender, self-sacrificing, and other such beautiful descriptions. This, for sure, is a biased and partial rendition. Overall, art suffers in the novel *To the Lighthouse* because the female contribution is rejected, and the female writer, Woolf, takes sides in a war of the sexes, undermining artistic wholesomeness.

Marcel Nyanchi's chapter, "Re-building Paradise: Islamic Ecosphere in Salman Rushdie's *The Satanic Verses*," situates us within the environmental humanities, highlighting the conflicts that ensue from human environmental interventions. Employing ecocritical theory informed by the perspectives of

Cheryll Glotfelty, Harold Fromm, and William Rueckert, Nyanchi discusses the different environmental conflicts in the novel from an Islamic point of view as delineated in the *Koran*. This religious text offers Allah's recommendations for man's interaction with nature to protect the ecosphere as a transcendental point between Allah and humans. Beginning with the coming of Islam to Jahilia and Titlipur, the main settings in the text, and ending with the opening of the Arabian Sea, the paper interrogates the successes and failures of different Islamic religious leaders in preserving the eco-cycle. The chapter hinges on the hypothesis that according to Islamic creation myths, paradise is the place wherein all matter, energy, and life are interconnected. Such unity can be preserved if one preserves the ecosystem by celebrating, meditating, and taking ethical actions through different art forms. Because of this intrinsic value, the chapter concludes that the *Koran* encourages every Muslim to resolve environmental conflicts by protecting his environment and the species that cohabitate.

PART TWO: LANGUAGE, CONFLICT CREATION AND CONFLICT RESOLUTION

In these essays on language, the role language plays in the creation, and the resolution of conflict is underscored as the essays reveal.

In Hans Fonka's essay, music is shown to be one of the domains where conflict is rife. Titled "Insults and Spear Words in Music: Cameroon Pidgincreole as a Battle Shield," the critic presents Cameroon Pidgincreole in music as both a conflict-generating and a conflict-resolution tool. With the use of Social Conflict Theory, the paper projects how Lapiro de Mbanga, through music, uses a specific variety of Cameroon Pidgincreole, namely, the Mboko variety, as a weapon to attack and also as a shield to hide himself against attack from a regime, which he tacks corrupt and repressive. The author holds that the choice of words used by Lapiro de Mbanga is sharp, direct, and provocative. Although it is good enough to create awareness, it also appeals to conflict as it invites repression of the musician whose voice is singled out. Fonka opines that the language used in the songs does not end at condemning systems; it attacks individuals, thus creating conflict that does not necessarily solve the problem intended to be exposed. This chapter concludes that so long as a language has an audience, it cannot be a cave to hide information, especially if the audience is interested in the message embedded in it.

Kiwoh Terence, in "Mitigating Linguistic Differences in Cameroon: The Role of Bilingual Education," presents issues of identity crises that have been manifested in a variety of ways and which have often hindered the integration of the two official language groups in Cameroon. The author profiles the state of national unity in Cameroon, examines various attempts made by government and private individuals to achieve harmony through bilingual education and proposes a bilingual education model that would contribute to building a new and acceptable official language identity. The paper ends with a firm conviction that adopting a "one class model" of bilingual education would go a long way to reshape loyalties to either French or English in Cameroon in the long run and strengthen integrated development.

As he probes evangelisation posters in Cameroon, Joseph Nkwain, in "The Power of Language in Persuasion: A Lexico-semiotic Reading of Evangelisation Crusade Posters in Cameroon," examines the role of language as a persuasive tool in evangelism crusades. He highlights the persuasive techniques and linguistic resources stakeholders employ in their design to lure potential crusaders and consolidate adherents' faith. It is anchored on the hypothetical premise that the power of language, especially in the domain of evangelisation, is mostly a measure of the effectiveness of the different persuasive techniques and the linguistic resources that underlie and reinforce related communicative acts. This shows that conflict is created in the religious domain when persuasive techniques are poorly used. The findings show that authors of posters employ a plethora of techniques ranging from association-based techniques such as beautiful people, bandwagon, symbolisem, and imagery.

Eunice Ngongkum, *University of Yaounde 1*
Hans Mbonwuh Fonka, *University of Bamenda*

List of Abbreviations

CPc	Cameroon Pidgincreole
CPE	Cameroon Pidgin English
CPDM	Cameroon Peoples' Democratic Movement
AAC	All Anglophone Conference
SCNC	Southern Cameroons National Council
SIL	Section d'initiation au langage *(Class one)*
CM1	Cour moyen 1 *(Class five)*
CM2	Cour Moyen 2 *(Class six)*
HOBEC	Horizone Bilingual Education Complex
ENIEG	Ecole nationale des instituteurs de l'enseignment general *(grade one teachers' Training College)*
GCE	General Certificate of Education

Part One

Literary Interrogations of Conflict

1

"The Agony of my Country"
Sierra Leone's Turbulent History in Syl Cheney-Coker's Poetry

EUNICE NGONGKUM

The functional premise of African literature is at the basis of its continuing dynamic relationship with the continent's history. African writers from across the generational gap like Chinua Achebe, Wole Soyinka, Ngugi wa Thiong'o, Nadine Gordimer, Niyi Osundare, Mongo Beti, Chimamanda Ngozi Adichie, and Zakes Mda, among others, have creatively engaged momentous events of African history from varying perspectives. The phenomenon of conflict, in its various forms, has been the bane of the continent since independence and remains a historical momentum informing the literature. Different ideological and aesthetic postures have been brought to bear on traumatic sites of violent conflict and war, laying bare not only the senseless aberration but, above all, the essence that lies beneath the "the contingent nature of historical fact" (Chreachain, 1996, p. 24). Cheney-Coker (2012), whose poetry I analyse in this essay, is one who has consistently responded to what he calls his country's "unique history, its sometimes unnecessary and painful explosions," engaging it in "a dialogue with its historical and social beginnings." These beginnings for the country have been pernicious, finally erupting into a full-blown war in 1991. How he does this in selected poems from *Concerto for an Exile* (1972), *The Graveyard also has Teeth* (1980), and *Blood in the Desert's Eyes* (1990), constitutes the focus of this essay.

Rooted in the understanding that literature can provide a much more intimate sense of history than historical fact itself, this essay analyses a selection of poems from Cheney-Coker's *Concerto for an Exile*, *The Graveyard also has Teeth*, and *Blood in the Desert's Eyes*, with the aim of situating Sierra Leone's civil war of 1991-2002 in a deeper historical context. The intention is to show that the war had deeper roots than sometimes acknowledged. From the perspective of the poems analysed herein, this essay argues that the seeds of the persistent conflict and eventual war lie beyond the country's diamonds, even though problems in the diamond sector did indeed contribute to the war (Boas, 2001; Keen, 2003; Reno, 2003 & Wigglesworth, 2008). The history and politics of the postcolony, the poetry indicates, inexorably led the country into violent civil strife. For those conversant with Sierra Leonean history, this may sound clichéd, but my argument is that the way in which the genre of poetry recreates and exposes the horrors that precipitated Sierra Leone into civil war makes for an interesting read. I agree with Chinua Achebe that in a time of crisis, the poetic genre is multifaceted enough for "making a statement, for bearing witness, for instigating a humane social and moral order, and for conscientising the reader to a better understanding of the corruption of power, and the patent often brazen, nature of evil" (Obiechina, 2002, p. 529).

New Historicism serves as a critical tool in my analysis. As a theory grounded in the intersection between art and history, it seeks to establish the relationship between works of art and their environment. According to Catherine Gallagher and Stephen Greenblatt (2000, p. 12), it is "concerned with finding the creative power that shapes a literary work *outside* the narrow boundaries in which it has hitherto been located, as well as *within* those boundaries." In New Historicism, the symbiotic relationship between art and history is a given, for all art is related to "the life world of the people from which it arises" (Gallagher & Greenblatt, 2000, p. 13). African writers recognise the interrelationship between art and historical consciousness in Africa. Achebe (1972, p. 7), for instance, says that African literature, like all other literature, "speaks of a particular place, evolves out of the necessities of its history, past and current and the destiny of its people." For Ngugi (1975, p. 39), "The writer's work is often an attempt to come to terms with the thing that has been, a struggle, as it were, to sensitively register his encounter with history, his people's history." Regarding the specific situation of his country, Cheney-Coker says that "the history of modern Sierra Leone is unlike no other West African nation and for a country so small; its politics has been very volatile. It does not leave a poet like me much choice than to comment on that agony" (Palmer & Cole, 2014, p. 35). Indeed, Cheney-Coker has spent much of his writing life commenting on the moments of danger facing post-independence Sierra Leone, battling with the forces of dehumanisation facing the country even as it moved inexorably unto war. How the poet does this in my selection is the major aim of this essay.

I argue that through a visionary and cautionary aesthetics, Cheney-Coker explores the historical antecedents of Sierra Leone's gradual decline into anarchy and civil war. Grounded in a deep knowledge of the history and socio-political culture of modern-day Sierra Leone, the poetry, written before the war, bears witness to the challenges of existence in post-independence Sierra Leone; challenges that eventually pushed the country into what the poet calls "a senseless war." The poetry holds up a critical mirror to society, warning about the deleterious socio-political and economic conditions that made for conflict. Poetry, for Cheney-Coker, represents a space for an imaginative engagement with the entity known as Sierra Leone, fostering social commitment and a need for active citizenship. To understand this engagement better, it is expedient to make forays into the history of a country once considered a pearl in Africa.

SIERRA LEONE'S CONFLICTS: HISTORICAL PERSPECTIVES

Sierra Leone owes its name to the Portuguese explorer, Pedro da Cintra who was the first to sight and map Freetown in the fifteenth century. This historical act exposed the country to the gory exercise of slavery and the slave trade in subsequent years. Its abolition in the early part of the nineteenth century propelled Sierra Leone into the limelight of international politics. Its capital, Freetown, was one of the first African cities to receive formerly enslaved people, as British and American philanthropists considered the area suitable for freed slaves to begin life anew. They thus provided the necessary material support for the initial development of this haven and closely monitored its growth and proper establishment. The only element uniting these people was their liberation from slavery; otherwise, they had very little in common culturally. This heterogeneity was instrumental in the formation of a Creole society, constructed largely on mimicry as European middle-class behaviour, attitudes, and tastes became defining cultural parameters fostering a sense of alienation from the indigenous population. This generated ethnic tensions, which contributed significantly to shaping conflict and violence. The British policy of indirect rule further exacerbated the situation. In a stifling tide of Eurocentrism, literate Sierra Leoneans (mainly Creoles) were sidelined in the management of affairs in favour of Europeans while a counter-elite, organised around existing chiefdom structures, was created to govern the colony pitting this elite against the Creoles. The turbulent political past of Sierra Leone is rooted in this unfortunate historical template.

At independence in 1961, Sierra Leone was thus far from being a united nation. Inheriting colonial legacies at the socio-political level resulted in the development of what Boas (2001, p. 697) has called an "extreme version of neo-patrimonial "politics" built on the need to secure the self through self-categorisation into self and others. Politics became a "personal and factional struggle aimed at controlling the state apparatus" (Boas, 2001, p. 698). The coup phenomenon and internecine conflict, hallmarks of contemporary Sierra Leonean life, are grounded in these fateful choices.

The country's economy depended on agriculture, diamond mining, and government employment. Diamond mining, seen as the major cause of the war, barely contributed one-fifth to government revenue thanks to a culture of smuggling, corruption, and greed. The bulk of the population bore the brunt of political ineptitudes and socio-economic inefficiencies. Poverty, disease, and squalor were the bane of the masses, while state resources rested in the hands of a small class whose economic role was complementary and subordinate to foreign capital. Even specific social services that facilitated the generation of wealth and economic development in a state were politically determined. The outcome of this desolate socio-political environment was widespread disaffection among the masses often expressed in military coups, civil unrest, and workers' strikes. Successive governments responded with repression, detentions, and executions of leading figures and the population. These responses only enflamed the situation culminating in the war of 1991.

From this brief overview, the historical heritage of Sierra Leone indicates that the civil war resulted from decades of ruthless political neglect, greed, and national mismanagement. Cheney-Coker's poetry provides a unique location to concretely x-ray these dystopian landscapes presenting how they were foundational to the civil war.

INTERROGATING CONFLICT LANDSCAPES: POETRY AS PROPHECY

Prophecy is rooted in a profound understanding of either the history or culture of the prophet. It includes his or her critical examination of society issuing forth from his or her perceptions of the socio-political environment. As the voice of vision of his time, the prophet can speak about the future because he is aware of what happened in the past, which if not taken into account will spell grim consequences for the future. An analysis of Cheney-Coker's poetry situates it within this framework. Grounded in the history of Sierra Leone, his visionary poetics is rooted in a critical ethos, truth saying and, in the capacity to anticipate a utopian society through a revolution. In the poems analysed here, different facets of Sierra Leone come under the critical lens of the poet. In a rich and varied poetic style, the poet lays bare the lacunae of the sociopolitical system, criticises negative attitudes, and expresses his anger and frustration in the face of social anomalies and aberrations. In many ways, as my analysis will show, the poems, in the words of Eustace Palmer and Ernest Cole, actually "anticipate the civil war" (2014, p. viii).

"Talons in the Flesh of my Country" (*The Graveyard*), "The Painting" (*The Blood*), "Volcano" and "Toilers" (*Concerto*) expose the ineptitude of successive governments in post-independence Sierra Leone and condemn the various outrages perpetrated by those in power against the masses. In these poems, Cheney-Coker defines the historical emergence of the bourgeoisified elite in power, paints a symbolic portrait of them, and details the disastrous effect of their monolithic rule.

In "Toilers," the foundation of this elite class lies in the peculiar historical circumstances of Sierra Leone. We are introduced to decolonisation in the opening lines. "A claustrophobia in my room because the sun is in orgasm there. / Then the dawn then the sickle the axe to smite me/because the sun has ejaculated the bad sperm of the drought" (Cheney-Coker, 1972, p. 14). "Claustrophobia" refers to the stifling model of governance available to Sierra Leone at independence, a model that gave room for authoritarianism and predation. The "sun in orgasm" suggests the aspirations of the citizenry at this juncture. Ironically, "the dawn" of independence produces "the bad sperm of the drought" as the masses discover that their toil, underlined in the images of "sickle" and "axe," is now the preserve of a kleptocracy obsessed with accumulating wealth and power.

> but I am no peasant farmer my name is government
> and I work in an air-conditioned office with ten telephones
> my days are limpid with brandy and ginger
> coursing slovenly at noon to my villa in the restricted zone
> proudly overlooking the sea
> and my dogs keep you off my luxuriant lawn
> inherited from the colonial master
> and my children are locked up in super elitist schools
> thus prohibiting the contagion of your disease (Cheney-Coker, 1972, p. 15).

The bureaucrat's speaking voice here is self-revealing in its bourgeois ethos. The rapidity with which these elite succeed to colonial power and privilege intimates its rootedness in capitalist culture.

> Yesterday it was independence celebrations

> and we threw in July fourteen as added attraction
> because ex-British or ex-French we have to pay our obedience
> howling the logistics about which was best colonial ourselves
> (Cheney-Coker, 1972, p. 15).

A mythic reference to crocodiles in the poem reveals the indifference of the elite to the plight of the masses; "now shamelessly I dare to mourn you with crocodile tears on paper nonsensical to you" (Cheney-Coker, 1972, p. 15). In Greek mythology, crocodiles were believed to shed tears over the hard necessity of killing other animals for food. The association further underlines the duplicity of these "beasts of brothers." The historical portrait of the power elite is yet palpable in "Talons in the Flesh of my Country," where the consequences of postcolonial politics are used to denounce the hegemonic status quo.

In the poem, Sierra Leone is now "a devastated landscape" and "a ghetto of silence" thanks to the politicians, "men of our dreams" who have simply become "men of our delusions." The oxymoron underlines the leadership's inability to deliver on its promises as it conversely 'rapes' the land and siphons its wealth into private pockets while paying lip service to development. A politics of emasculation stifles counter-hegemonic voices plunging the nation into "a ghetto of silence." Images related to devouring, raping, and eating like "talons, "cut-throats," and "lizards" establish these elites as greedy parasites whose ethos is what Bayart (1986) has called, in another context, "La politique du ventre." Bayart's concept designates a situation where elites gravitate towards the state for material gain. Zack-Williams (2012, p. 144) notes that in post-independence Sierra Leone, the ruling elite introduced "A whole network of client-patron relationships…premised on state access to sufficient revenue in order to placate clients." The poet's rage at this turn of events is underlined through appropriate diction and realistic detail.

> …my mouth trembles with my verse
> seeing their treachery walking
> arm-in-arm with justice the life howling
> like a brochure of stamps and leones
> the monolithic arrogance of power
> they stuff themselves with for now! (Cheney-Coker, 1972, p. 53).

The verb "trembles" and the personification of treachery "walking arm-in-arm with justice" underline the speaker's anger at the subordination of the judiciary by state power. This situation constitutes part of the arsenal of personalised rule referred to by Morton Boas in precedent pages. Personalised rule employs the judiciary and other instruments of the state to advance the leader's rationale. This may be why Marcella Macauley notes in "International Actors and Democracy Promotion in Post-Conflict Sierra Leone: Time for Stock-Taking" that the 'soft' nature of the Sierra Leonean state "resulted in the lack of access to justice." She insists that being an arm of the state, the judiciary could "not act against the interest of the centre" (2012, pp. 30-31). It maintained the kleptocracy in power while oppressing the masses. This poem, from Macauley's observations, is thus clear about the historic fault lines of the underlying conflictual situation in Sierra Leone, rooted not only in the genesis of the country but also in its polity.

For a sensitive artist like Cheney-Coker, poetic commitment demands that he "write[s] about these beasts/about these waters," so that the people can be conscientized about the reality of things and seek change. This is the essence of committed poetry, namely, "addressing those in power and those who [can] influence those in power," as Peter Horn intimates elsewhere (1994, p. 49). Images of toxicity such as "deadly contagion," "bile," "toxins" delineate the detrimental mode of governance hinged on what Zack-Williams (2012, p. ix) calls "chronic kleptomania." Paradoxically the outcome for Sierra Leoneans, who drink of the "precious waters" of personalised rule, irrespective of class, is violence and destruction, as the civil war subsequently demonstrated. As far back as the eighties, when this poem was published, Cheney-Coker had foreseen the disastrous outcome of the mode of governance in post-independence Sierra Leone and called attention to it. It was a political model that, in the nineteen-eighties, was to reduce Sierra Leone to a "weak" or "failed" state - one in which the restoration of effective central institutions was at best problematic. International Financial Organisations intervened and only aggravated the situation with structural adjustment programmes. "The Painting" (*The Blood*) x-rays this episode in Sierra Leonean history through allusion and analogy.

The poem begins by alluding to Francesco Goya's painting of Saturn devouring his son; an allegory of the situation in Spain where the country consumed its citizens in wars and revolutions. This allusion is drawn from its Euro-cultural frame of reference to perform the critical task of highlighting Sierra Leone on the brink of self-destruction and decay thanks to flawed and violent statecraft:

> When the undertaker had measured the corpse
> he made a coffin fit for the body of a dwarf
> when the peninsula woke up one morning

> it received a gift in the form of a massacre
> when the vultures arrived drawn to the country
> by the news of the drought they found
> Saturn devouring his children (Cheney-Coker, 1990, p. 14).

Analogy here in reference to mortuary servicing is effective in underlining the country's recourse to international financial institutions at the time. As a result of bureaucratic corruption and clientelist politics, government expenditure surpassed income, and Sierra Leone was declared a heavily indebted country. The "undertaker" is the elite who have impoverished the country declaring it a "dwarf." This image conjures up the malfunctioning of the organs of the body that has led to an abnormally short height. Patronage politics and widespread corruption severely limited the country's development offensive leading to the invitation of the "vultures." The vulture image delineates the predatory nature of global capitalist institutions that ostensibly come to help the country out of its "drought" with structural adjustment programs that only worsen the economic and political state of affairs, while enriching the institutions in question. The poet's position is that, before the arrival of these global bodies, the greed of the elite, labelled "its cannibal instincts," together with destructive ethnic politics pushed the country to the brink of economic and social despair. The politicians' indifference to the country's plight is likened to someone "devouring" their "own children." The mythic reference to Saturn, the Roman god of agriculture given to orgies and other excesses, aptly emphasises the destructive essence of monolithic power and its characteristic greed.

The poem next describes what transpires at the undertaker's as a corpse is prepared for burial. The slight variation qualifying the undertaker as "rich," simply underlines the fact that he has enriched himself from the business of arranging corpses for interment. This image may point to the politician who undertakes to cater for the country but whose "meanness" has led him to exploit the resources of the state for his own ends. Symbolic references to Sierra Leone as "a dwarf" and "a corpse" are significant in the context of post-independence Sierra Leone. Zack-Williams (2012) notes in his introduction to *When the State Fails* that at independence, Sierra Leone was poised to be among the prominent countries in Africa by virtue of its natural resources and enduring institutions. All these factors which could have led the country on the path of social justice and economic prosperity were punctured at the very beginning of the democratic experiment by tribalism, patronage networks, and political egotism. The rejection of the country's "weak" state status by the masses is evident in these lines

> this corpse wants no eulogy it wants no funeral song
> it scorns remembrance it wants no tomb
> but if they put it in a pauper's grave
> this corpse will rise, and walking across the cemetery
> will strangle the rich man in his grave;
> for this corpse is my country! (Cheney-Coker, 1990, p. 14).

This vivid presentation of a corpse, ready to rise from its grave and "strangle" the rich man in his grave, is visionary in perspective. The Sierra Leone conflict was already predicted in these lines, and as the poet has said, in another context, "Many years ago, I saw the disingenuousness of the educated classes; their wanton disregard of the populace… and … predicted a storm. The rest, we might say, is history" (Cole, 2012, p. 142).

To suggest that the rich man is also in "a grave" is to underscore the moral bankruptcy of the hegemony which is "dead" to the plight of the masses. The poet uses the personal pronoun "my" to convey his emotional pain at this sad state of affairs. He equally envisions change with the uprising of the masses. The use of death-related metaphors emphasises the destructive essence of monolithic rule which did not only plunge the economy into distress, as this poem suggests, but also failed to provide space for alternative voices. This situation found an outlet in the frequent and rampant violent upheavals, political victimisation, and executions that became a hallmark of political life. This is the premise on which poems like "Concerto for an Exile" (Concerto, 1972, p. 20) and "Volcano" (Concerto, 1972, pp. 21-22) are built.

"Concerto for an Exile," provides the title for Cheney-Coker's first poetry collection. In an interview with Brown (1981, p. 56), he underlines the historical antecedents of the poem: ""Concerto for an Exile" came about as a result of the execution of Brigadier John Bangura who was Army Chief of Staff. He was executed in 1971." Brigadier John Bangura toppled the Margai government and installed Siaka Stevens in power. He soon discovered that Stevens' government was a self-serving comprador regime at the service of global finance. He staged another coup to overthrow it, failed, and was executed.

Generally in this poem, as in "Volcano", imagery is effective in decrying the violent political landscape which is the result of the actions of "fratricidal brothers/whose lust has made the Sierra a volcano too bloody…." Surrealist imagery, "And the guns roared on/in Sierra Leone/to plunder the tree of agony in my soul," reinforces the dramatic opening; "The news of the coups the bullets in my soul! / I plunge into the streets holding the dead in my head." The political upheavals are so deadly that the country is now "a boulevard of corpses." Hyperbole, reinforced by apt diction, "bloody," "executioners," "decalcified," "slit their bellies," "eruption tearing my country apart," "ravaged Sierra Leonean earth" underscore the violent political culture of post-independence Sierra Leone that was a major cause of the civil strife. These upheavals are further captured in landscape imagery in "Volcano" where the metaphor of an active volcano, is employed to underline not only the constant political turmoil, but also the imminent revolt of the oppressed.

Cheney-Coker does not only indict the predatory governance logic's prime role in the civil conflict but also examines the contribution made by social dissatisfaction to it. As it were, the structural problems engendered by corrupt and inept statecraft led to increased grievances among the people. Christensen (2008, p. 55) says, to this effect, that "the poor and disenfranchised in Sierra Leone had genuine grievances that were manipulated by the insurgents for their own ends." These grievances were located in an intersecting set of local and global actors keen on benefiting from the country's diamonds much to the exclusion of the masses. Many Sierra Leoneans joined the war because they felt excluded from the benefits accruing from the country's mineral wealth extraction. This perspective argues for the reading of the civil war as part of a larger drama of social exclusion; exclusion evident in the masses' abject misery, suffering, poverty, and squalor. Cheney-Coker recreates this world in "Nausea" (*The Graveyard*), "Myopia" (*Concerto*), "Poet amongst those who are Poets" (*The Graveyard*), and "The Blood in the Desert's Eyes" (*The Blood*). The manner in which he juxtaposes suffering and the rage of the poor at their plight, seems to indicate that a growing reduction in purchasing power, malnutrition, vulnerability to endemic diseases, and hopelessness was instrumental in fuelling the conflict. "Nausea" is built on the vision of the world of the oppressed as apathetic.

In the poem, the persona identifies with suffering humanity in his context. This is a world in which a "mother chews a thousand pieces of cocaine/to fill her stomach's void" and the "singing mulatress," living in the shanty nurses "her son/in whose eyes she reads the hungry patterns of death." The predatory governance logic is underlined as the root cause of this situation, as the plight of these characters is "wrought by those who have never sorrowed/by those who have never known pain/by those who have never died once" (Cheney-Coker, 1980, p. 59). Structural and ideational parallelisms stress the speaker's anger at this class that "others" the masses because of political and economic privilege. It renders life nightmarish for the poor and paradoxically thinks money and power will spare it sorrow, pain, and death. The satiric intention is clear as these realities are common to all men regardless of class.

The peasants, whose labour builds the country but who ironically are "drenched" on "rainy mornings," "shivering in their emaciated bones/along the boulevards of misery," are the subject of "Myopia" (*Concerto*, 1972, p. 38). Surrealist imagery accentuates the paradox of suffering amidst plenty, and the awful spectacle of a country's human and material resources being systematically depleted by a materialistic class. These are the issues that arouse the poet's ire.

> the boulevards of this country
> are railway tracks in my heart
> a train of anguish runs on them
> rage corollary of hunger (Cheney-Coker, 1972, p. 38).

The conceits in this extract express the mental agony at seeing these contradictions in an otherwise rich country like Sierra Leone. Anger in this context becomes a legitimate impulse at the fact that the country's wealth has become the preserve of an insensitive few.

"Poet among those who are also poets" (*The Graveyard*, 1980, p. 67), employs techniques of documentation and cinematography to present varying scenes of suffering and misery in Freetown. As the persona drives around "its dirty streets," his poetic lens captures with realism and matter-of-factness, the frustrated man committing suicide, another chewing kola nut to check his hunger, and yet another "crouching half dying under a giant cotton tree." The scene shifts to the presidential palace where a man is "shrieking with a stream of saliva running down his face" and "a beggar goes by shouting he has been robbed."

The scene turns to the women where one of them is "screaming raped by a bureaucrat" while "a childless harlot is beaten by another with kids." At the shanty, there is no water because "the women have ruined the toilets" and another woman confesses her greed of selling her daughter. The children are next in focus with "one child" driven to school in "a limousine unmarked/ while the classmates walk on all ten." At the hospital, we are told there is "commotion because two children/have been bitten over at the garbage dump." This image of "life seen driving around Freetown" realistically demonstrates how human beings have been reduced to the level of animals by a system that degrades, dehumanises, and destroys. By systematically focusing on men, women, and children, the poet deplores the all-embracing effect of monolithic rule. Parallelism and repetitions in the poem highlight the theme and attitude. Juxtaposition, occurring between the beggar standing by the presidential palace and the child driven to school while others walk, calls attention to the gulf between the masses and the elite which the poet condemns.

One outstanding aspect of Cheney-Coker's vision is the anticipation of an end to all forms of oppression suffered by the poor. Many of the characters in his poetry are aware of their predicament and simultaneously prepared to rise up in defiance against the evil system. In "The Blood in the Desert's Eyes" (Cheney-Coker, 1990, p. 5) for instance, the poet anticipates the revolt of the downtrodden through an illumination of the present. The spotlight here is on the miners who represent the dispossessed. The poet-speaker observes them coming up out of the mine, "bearing their universal ash/ the black bread of life." The enjambment is used to good effect for it emphasises the fact that the diamond ash is universally profitable, and expected to provide a lasting and lifetime fulfilment for these workers as captured in the biblical allusion "bread of life." Ironically, however, the world of the miners is simply "turned upside down" because these "masters of the dew" are dispossessed. Images of suffering conveyed through diction like "longing," "neighing," "uncreative longing," "thoracic longing," "proboscis flexing the want," and "stoic," among others, underline the extent to which suffering is so much a part of the world of the toilers that, it is likened to an ulcer that festers and corrupts the whole body.

The image "laudanum of life" reinforces the suffering that has become analogous with the oppressed. Yet, these miners do not seem to be condemned to a life of futility and despair. We find them in the poem expressing their "centrifugal rage" against their plight. The journey image (The miners' journey to the heart of the earth and back) highlights the fact that the seeming cycle of drudgery will eventually come to an end. In effect, we find the men coming "up to earth" in stanza one, looking "melancholic and brooding." After observing their world in stanza two, they go "back from earth" in stanza three, "enormous with rage." They actively and patiently prepare their revolt; patience analogous with the diurnal occurrence of the sun captured in the image "the mocking grandfather sun." The understanding here is that as long as the sun rises daily, there is every reason to believe that patience will be rewarded in the end and that the desired change will come. The potential for revolt is present, as captured in the image of "the blood in the desert's eyes."

The peasants are the eyes of the desert, in the sense in which the country has been rendered sterile by the powers that be, and peasants are the ones enlivening it by their toil. "Blood" is an image of destruction and therefore emphasises the fact that retributive violence by the oppressed is a legitimate impulse against exploitation and misery. Cheney-Coker identifies with this miner "who breaks his bread with me." In this way, he demonstrates his pain at seeing them suffer at the hand of exploitative power.

Symbolism operates in much of Cheney-Coker's poetry to underline his revolutionary vision. The symbolic "blood in the desert's eye" becomes a motif of the revolutionary potential of the peasants. The conditions in pre-war Sierra Leone made the country "desert" and the people lethargic, yet like cacti which thrive in desert surroundings, the peasants have the dynamic energy, the "blood" to bring about a change in their circumstances. But what the poet seems to prefer is a symbolic healing of the spiritual blindness of these ones so that they may fully exploit their potential for action. Cheney-Coker seems to hint here at the concept of the historic backwardness of the African peasant, drawn and used by the forces of imperialism to maintain the black man in servitude. It is a mentality inherited and cultivated by the comprador class against the downtrodden in pre-war Sierra Leone. This is the central theme of "The Walk of the Blind" (Cheney-Coker, 1990, p. 73), where the peasants are shown as "blind" to the real causes of their predicament, but seen as a group that can be positively conscientized for revolutionary action. Rhetorically, the speaker tries to imagine the outcome of such a possible awakening of these poor:

> But if these victims of our neglect should moan
> if these abandoned promises reared their ugly heads
> to demand a knife to our throats, the justice
> for failing to be our brother's keepers, of having poisoned
> the sun to deprive them of seeing...
> if they lost their blindness what price their revenge?
> (Cheney-Coker, 1990, p. 73)

As a collectivity, the total vision of the Sierra Leonean, and by extension, the African peasant has been shattered since the encounter between Africa and Europe. The central myth of 'groupness' has been destroyed by a civilisation of individualism animating the elite. In the poem above, there is the need to review the status quo and revalorise the position of the peasant in the context of the revolution. Revolt begins by rejecting the image of self as a scattered group of "blind" people, incapable of attending to their predicament. The poet revives that central myth of togetherness around a common theme of suffering at the hand of the "fratricidal brother." He imbues these masses with a consistent revolutionary character. Pitted against their oppressors, through the technique of juxtaposition, the speaker underscores the reasons and sum total of the efforts of the entire revolutionary experience of the downtrodden.

CONCLUSION

This analysis has shown that Cheney-Coker's poetry, in the context of post-independence Sierra Leone, can be classed as prophecy. The poems demonstrate a keen sense of history, a history which unfortunately seems to be embedded in endemic violence. They underline the various indignities suffered by the downtrodden at the hands of those dubbed "these thieves of brothers." The rulers and the structures of imperialism are targets of Cheney-Coker's satire. His disillusionment with the ruling elite is delineated in animal imagery. A good number of poems x-ray the incompetence of the particular political strategies in the country. The obsession with the political indicates that poor governance was the leading cause of the war. In discussing the world of the oppressed, on the other hand, we find a preponderance of disease imagery, images of violence, deprivation and want, among others. In both cases, language and poetic form concatenate to underscore the singular circumstances that informed the Sierra Leonean conflict.

Cheney-Coker actually anticipates the possible outcome of the disappointments and frustrations of the oppressed group, an outcome that was the civil war, even if the trajectory of the war turned into an orgy of killings and destruction of horrendous proportions. The poet sensitises the oppressed population to take individual or collective action against greedy and unconscionable leadership. In the absence of "channels of dissent" (Brown, 1981, p 56) in the country, poetry becomes valid not only in speaking out against the outrages perpetrated by those in power, but also in awakening the suffering people to the reality of their predicament. As an aesthetic experience, the poetry offers valuable insights into political events and experiences that largely contributed to the civil war.

REFERENCES

Achebe, C. (1975). The Role of the Writer in a New Nation. In G.D. Killam (Ed.), *African Writers on African Writing.* (pp. 7-13). Heinemann.

Babatunde, A. Z-W. (1999). Sierra Leone: the Political Economy of Civil War, 1991-98. *Third World Quarterly.* 20 (1), 143-162.

Babatunde, A. Z-W. (2012a). Multilateral Intervention in Sierra Leone's Civil War: Some Structural Explanations. In Z-W. Tunde (Ed.). *When the State Fails. Studies*

on Intervention in the Sierra Leone Civil War (pp.13-30). Pluto Press.
Babatunde, A. Z-W. (2012b). Preface. In Z-W. Tunde (Ed.), *When the State Fails. Studies on Intervention in the Sierra Leone Civil War* (pp. i-xi). Pluto Press.
Bayart, J-F. (1989). *L'état en afrique. La politique du ventre.* Fayard.
Brown, S. (1981). A Poet in Exile. *Index on Censorship* 10 (6), 55-57.
Cheney-Coker, S. (1972). *Concerto for an Exile: Poems.* Heinemann.
Cheney-Coker, S. (1990). *The Blood in the Desert's Eyes.* Heinemann.
Cheney-Coker, S. (1980). *The Graveyard Also Has Teeth.* London: Heinemann.
Cheney-Coker, S. (2012). The Second Coming of the Bellwether: Contemporary Sierra Leone and its March towards Modernization in the Age of Twitter, Instant Banking and Other Transitions. http://awoko.org/2012/02/02/the-second-coming-of-the-bellwether/. 2012.
Chréacháin, F. N. (1996). History & Radical Aesthetics: A Study of Festus Iyayi's Heroes. In J. D. Eldred and J. Marjorie (Eds.), *New Trends and Generations in African Literature Today 20*, 14- 24. James Currey.
Cole, E. (2012). Interview with Syl Cheney-Coker. Email Interview.
Gallagher, C. & Greenblatt S. (2000). *Practicing New Historicism.* U of Chicago Press.
Horn, P. (1994). *Writing my Reading. Essays on Literary Politics in South Africa.* Rodopi.
Keen, D. (2003). Greedy Elites, Dwindling Resources, Alienated Youth: The Anatomy of Protracted Violence in Sierra Leone. In *IPS.* 2, 67-94.
Matthew J. C. (2008). Enslaving Globalization: Civil War and Modernity in Sierra Leone. In *The Global South.* 2 (2), 54-74).
Morton, B. (2001). Liberia and Sierra Leone: Dead Ringers? The Logic of Neopatrimonial Rule. In *Third World Quarterly.* 22 (5), 697-723.
Macaulley, M. (2012). International Actors and Democracy Promotion in Post- Conflict Sierra Leone: Time for Stock-Taking. In Z-W. Tunde (Ed.), *When the State Fails. Studies on Intervention in the Sierra Leone Civil War.* (pp.31-64), Pluto Press.
Ngugi, W. T. (1975). *Homecoming.* Essays on African and Caribbean Literature, Culture and Politics. Heinemann.
Obiechina, E. (2002). Poetry As Therapy: reflections on Achebe's *Christmas in Biafra and Other Poems." Callaloo.* 25 (2), 527-559).
Palmer, E. & Cole, E. (Eds.). (2014). *Emerging Perspectives on Syl Cheney-Coker.* Africa World Press.
Reno, W. (2003). Political Networks in a Failing State: The Roots and Future of Violent Conflict in Sierra Leone. *International Politics and Society.* 2, 29-43.
Wigglesworth, G. (2008). The End of Impunity? Lessons from Sierra Leone. *International Affairs (Royal Institute of International Affairs 1944-2004.* 84 (4), 809-827

2

Bob Marley and the Discourse of Conflict

KELVIN NGONG TOH

The human race is heterogeneous, made of different cultures, identities and races. These differences have fundamentally built barriers that separate people and group them into "us" and "they" with the instinct to protect and enclose the "us" (Said, 1993). In order to protect "us," the gaze on "they" has not been very accommodating since "us" is humane and civilised while "they" is inhumane and uncivilised. This purist outlook of communities has created conflict as each binary projects itself "sacred." The struggle to keep one's community "sacred" is fostered more in seeing the other as "profane," and this "difference" only leads to friction and factionalism among people.

In the words of Jeong (2008), "conflict dates from the beginning of human history and will probably never end. Our survival on this planet hinges on how we manage the various features of conflict fuelled not only by seemingly incompatible interests and values but also by hostilities" (p. 3). Conflicts exist as a human phenomenon, making it part of the human world. However, the effects of conflict reveal that humans struggle to deal with the condition whose by-products can be otherwise, ultimately leading to shame, disgrace, and regrets. Nevertheless, the communities, races and nations no sooner find themselves in the same kind of fighting.

Conflict questions the rationality of people and the supposedly strong desire to live together. Though the landmarks of conflict resolution and crisis management lie in "neutrality," it seems, as I will discuss in this chapter, that the artist (literary artist, painter, filmmaker, musician, sculptor, and architect), as a crisis indicator and resolver, can hardly be defined as neutral. This is why I discuss Bob Marley's songs as compositions that the artist uses to reveal conflicts.

What Marley does in his music as one who takes sides with the "people" has been the significant standpoint of many intellectuals who argue that art should be on the side of the oppressed and not the oppressors (Ngugi, 1982 & Said, 1996). Ngugi and Said, like many others, have argued that it is only when the artist and/or intellectual takes the side of the "people" that their art and ideology are political and regarded as committed. While I have queries about this limited scope of political art and committed art, I argue that Marley's music subscribes to this logic. This position is relevant in this study because all conflicts have a sociocultural root that causes their ambiguities. Sandole (2007) affirms that "whether an enraged individual is committing an act of "warfare" or "terrorism" against his or her perception of the Oppressor or Enemy may be largely a question of culturally based construction" (p. 1). Situating conflict in contemporary times caused by sociocultural associations is also sustained by Huntington (1993, p. 22), who opines:

> It is my hypothesis that the fundamental source of conflict in this new world will not be primarily ideological or primarily economic. The great divisions among humankind and dominating source of conflict will be cultural. Nation states will remain the most powerful actors in world affairs, but the principal conflicts of global politics will occur between nations and groups of different civilizations.

Huntington's defence of the new wave of conflict in the post-Cold War era shifting it to conflict of cultures and civilisations is relevant. Huntington's emphasis on cultural tensions at the heart of conflict is worth considering. Therefore, a proper understanding of conflict involves an in-depth knowledge of the psychology of human behavioural patterns and the social construction of the community (Jeong, 2008). Without necessarily pining this chapter down to the Jamaican experience (the songs handle universal issues; the blackness of the Black Man and poor post-independence leadership, issues beyond Marley's Jamaican homeland), the analysis focuses on the dynamics of the artistic world and the techniques that the artist uses to interpret and represent the different conflicts that characterise postcolonial Jamaica, the Caribbean and the black world at large.

THE GENRE IN PERSPECTIVE

Music is generally considered an expressive art form which manifests a society's rich cultural diversity and strength. Music is a cultural and societal artefact expressed through the artist's creative imagination. Another thing that makes music an exciting and potent art is that it transcends all boundaries and speaks to the minds and souls of even the novice of music literacy. Therefore, organised sound can meet humankind's emotional and psychic aspirations without barriers. For this reason, musicians are also known as people of culture. In the view of Gilroy (1993), music constitutes an essential aspect of the Black Atlantic culture, both contemporary and modernist. To better our understanding of the Black Atlantic, Gilroy (1993, p. 73) writes:

> They [black musicians] are modern because they have been marked by their hybrid, creole origins in the West, because they have struggled to escape their status as commodities and the position within the cultural industries it specifies, and because they are produced by artists whose understanding of their own position relative to the racial group and of the role of art in mediating individual creativity with social dynamics is shaped by a sense of artistic practice as an autonomous domain either reluctantly or happily divorced from the everyday life.

This is a good description of Reggae music – the genre of music that Marley played – which was born in the ghettos of Jamaica (Jamaica was a British colony which gained independence in 1962). The country has had poor leaders, and that has made daily life to be characterised by hardship and the music's originators are usually referred to as the "rude boys" or the *sufferahs* (Forest, 1985; Lokaisingh-Meighoo, 2001). It is historically agreed that Reggae, especially from Jamaica, began to reach an international audience in the 1970s.

Marley's music is from the ghetto and reflects much of Trench Town life, where he grew up in Kingston. His music, in every sense, Black Atlantic music, is also the music of a hybrid culture (Chevannes, 2001). It is one musical genre whose hybrid nature is multifaceted. First, it is born in the popular culture tradition and violates many Jamaican musical principles. Forest (1985, p. 77) records that "This type of thing [Reggae] was not at all what the local bourgeoisie had in mind for their "post-independence" Jamaican culture." The fact is clear that the ruling class of this Nation-State was in conflict with the "rude boys" who began this kind of music. This is because the "rude boys" were considered leftist, and critical of the government as they identified primarily with the poor people and ghetto life in Kingston, the capital of Jamaica.

Secondly, Reggae music has strong ties with Jamaican culture and religion. The religious bases of the Rastafarian religion to which Marley's Reggae adhered could be traced from the Queen of Sheba's relationship with King Solomon. Ras Tafari, also known as Emperor Haile Selassie, will become the divine image of the Rastafarian religion, which is a "mixing" of Christianity,

Judaism, Islam and Ethiopian cultures. One characteristic of Marley's Reggae is the blend between spirituality and his reactionary/revolutionary response to all forms of injustice in society. Marley is referred to as one of the Rastafarian prophets because Rastafarian religious ideologies principally guide his music.

Reggae music is highly instrumental, with guitars and drums being dominant. The uniqueness of the music is first seen in the dominance of the rhythmic guitar, usually determining the timing of 4/4 (quarter time). In terms of vocals, it follows the solo/chorus technique, and in Marley's case, some of the songs are solos like the case of "Redemption Song." Three kinds of reggae have been identified – the Ska, Rock Steady and the Dub. The Ska is quick and lively. The Rock Steady is slower, and the Dub that came up in the 1970s is generally a remix and uses a lot of modern musical technology.

Reggae artists generally keep dreadlocks in the tradition of the Rastafarian. It is also asserted that most of them, especially those who belong to the Rastafarian religion, smoke Ganja (marijuana) as a religious ritual and as a source of inspiration. Reggae is so connected to the Rastafarian that it is hard to see a Reggae artist and separate him physically and ideologically from the religion (even though it is true that not all Reggae artists are Rastafarians). Like the religion, most Reggae artists see themselves as liberators and freedom fighters. They see themselves as Zionists fighting against the oppression that is coming from Babylon.

BOB MARLEY: THE CONFLICT INDICATOR

In this section, the focus is on Marley's effort to highlight what brings about conflict, especially in multiracial and post-independence societies. This is because conflict is a human activity with social, cultural, identity and religious roots. Jeong (2008) rightly opines that "managing and preventing conflict begins with understanding the source of the social struggle. We can explain the basis of conflict and related behavior in terms of human motivation, patterns of social interaction, and institutions" (p. 43). It then becomes clear that if a conflict situation is not thoroughly studied and understood from its sociocultural and political origins, the problem may not be resolved satisfactorily, and cosmetic solutions to such problems only postpone the problems.

Marley's music is born from a society that has learnt to live in conflict. DeLoughrey (2007) asserts that the Caribbean has a violent history of colonialism and a complex layering of native and diaspora populations. Marley's music addresses this kind of society as he continuously stands against all forms of injustice that naturally breed conflict. Stephens (1999, p. 13) adroitly states that "Bob Marley's music, most immediately about black liberation, has been reframed by the singer and his corporate producers and delivered to global, multi-ethnic audience, which in turn 'reads' these texts in ways often far removed from their 'racial context.'" Stephens's findings show that Marleyian art has crossed the borders of Jamaica and the Caribbean and today is heard worldwide. This universalist outpouring of Marleyian art only fosters the fact that injustice and violence are universal concerns.

Marley's concern for denouncing what is wrong in society makes him a conflict exposer. In this sense, this study describes him as a humanist and a philosopher because his music also ponders the human condition. One of the ideologies Marley radically stands against is Capitalism and its modernist spirit of individualism, which has reduced humanity into what Marley terms the "rat race." "Rat Race," as a soundtrack, opens with a musical introduction with accentuated notes at the beginning of every measure, and the first lyrical line is "Ya too rude." This strong musical sound and the very opening lyric already reveal that the song is not focused on any form of politeness and does not go for any niceties. The tone of the song is vituperative:

> Oh, it's a disgrace
> To see the human-race
> In a rat race.

The dominant consonant and the [s] sound in the above lines, the end-rhyme patterns foster the strong message of the lines built on the metaphor of the rat, to which, unfortunately, the human race has been reduced. This is because, like the rat, the human race has turned to individualism, translated in the greed and selfishness that the human race almost celebrates as a modern and postmodern way of living. Taylor, a critique of modernist ways, says this of individualism; "[I] mean by these features of our contemporary culture and society that people experience as a loss or a decline, even as our civilization 'develops" (1991, p. 1). In individualism or greed, Taylor sees the decline of the community and communal in Man. In Taylor's view, the post-humanist tendency only pushes humanity into a lonely space and his/her complete reliance on self and machines. Taylor sees such a human development as a malaise leading to the decline and destruction of humanity.

In the rat image, one finds the very elements of humanity such as love, peace, happiness and togetherness, losing out to greed. Selfishness, the desire to own, profit-making and more importantly, the fact that humanity, in the spirit of inventing, is shifting increasingly into individualism. Marley articulates that:

> When you think of peace and safety
> A sudden destruction.
> Collective security for surety, Ye-ah.

The paradox in these lines is that the effort to build leads humanity to destroy. More and more, the agencies created to end conflict since 1919 have done very little to check conflicts among nations, tribes and even men. Part of what caused these conflicts is that humanity has not yet checked its greed. For this reason, humanity begins to look for solutions to problems it creates.

Besides individualism, the polarised society – constructed on difference, race and class – is fundamental in Marley's art. This binary opposition is a significant source of conflict in human society. In most of Marley's music, racism is the primary source of conflict in multiracial societies. What is absurd about racist identification and differentiation is that it is an ideology that is constructed fundamentally on "skin colour," as Tizard and Phoenix (2002, p. 8) claim and holds that the "white race" associates superiority to itself. In one of his philosophical pieces entitled "War," Marley sees racism or racial injustice as a significant cause for conflicts in multiracial societies. The lyrics of the song open thus:

> Until the philosophy which hold one race superior
> And another
> Inferior
> Is finally
> And permanently
> Discredited
> And abandoned –
> Everywhere is war –
> Me say war.

Marley judges racism as evil. It separates people based on the colour of their skin, which is a basic abuse of human rights because the colour of the skin cannot determine who one is. Within the context of Marley's verse – an adaptation of Emperor Haile Selassie's speech to the United Nations in the mid-1970s – white racism that remains one of the leading ideological promoters for the trans-Atlantic slave trade and colonialism is seriously attacked. Marley signals injustice in his lyrics that characterises the multiracial societies of the Caribbean and the world. Here, Marley particularly attacks institutionalised racism. This is clear because racial laws and regulations have plunged societies into violence, threat and conflict, governed by hate (Bolaffi et al., 2003).

The lyrics are a complete rebuff of institutionalised racism, especially enshrined by white supremacist ideology. It is important to stress that this speech by Emperor Haile Selassie, poetically adopted and transmitted in music, testifies to the extent to which institutional racism had threatened peace in the twentieth century. Fredrickson (2002, p. 99) writes to this effect that "White supremacy attained its fullest ideological and institutional development in the southern United States between 1890s and the 1950s, and in South Africa between the 1910s and the 1980s, but especially after 1948. Antisemitism, of course reached its horrendous climax in Nazi Germany between 1933 and 1945." Understanding Marley's upbringing in Jamaica, where racism was/is one of the leading ideologies; Marley submits that where racism exists, war is inevitable.

In the lyrics, Marley sings of the meanness and ignobility of the regimes that had built their state ideology on the colour line.

> And until the ignoble and unhappy regimes
> That hold our brothers in Angola,
> In Mozambique
> South Africa
> Sub-human bondage
> Have been toppled,
> Utterly destroyed –
> Well everywhere is war –
> Me say war.

Besides meanness to all who practice racism, the ideology as Marley states, cannot render its followers happy. In other words, the sarcastic tone of the song also preaches the doom and misery of those perpetrating racism. He enumerates countries under the yoke of racialised governments as a sign that makes the artist also an activist for freedom. Even then, the choice of words that we find in the lines above, such as: "toppled/destroyed," also shows Marley's Fanonian view that the liberation of a people can only come through violence since no people are put in most bondage state peacefully (Fanon, 2004). The adverse effects of racism have led to its collapse as an institutionalised policy in most states that adopted it from the United States to South Africa (Fredrickson, 2002). Marley's music is still relevant in that multiracial societies continue to live with this divide, with the white race still self-claiming superiority. Moreover, violence and community conflict continue to rise. The case of Charlottesville, USA, in 2017 is one instance in our time. Even the blame theory used by the then United States President Donald J. Trump only shows his covering up of the white supremacist cults, and as Marley puts it, such a position will lead to war.

"War" is one song that Marley's anti-racist belief is so strong, and his commitment to fighting it is unequivocal. The song seems to give no room for any dialogue or peaceful gradualism. Marley is categorical that even with tension and war, racism especially, the injustice against Africans must end. He concludes with the call that

> Until that day,
> The African continent
> Will know no peace.
> We Africans
> Will fight,
> We find it necessary
> As we know we shall win
> As we are confident.

Any quick observer listening to these lines knows that Marley has declared war and in the war, he hopes that Africans will win. Of course, this war only enforces the fact that as racism continues to thrive, conflict will continue to abound, and more specifically, the black race and Africans will continue to fight. We observe that though white racism against black people is no longer institutional in and out of the African continent, black people in Europe and the United States of America are still living in violent situations. Surprisingly, no African president has condemned racialised acts against black people in the United States and Europe, including the Charlottesville incident. Marley sees this fight against racial injustice as a fight that black people must continue to fight, for it is evident that they (black people) will win. In the last lines of the song, the singer chants:

> We Africans will fight
> We fight it necessary
> As we know we shall win
> As we are confident in the victory.

The underlying principle here is that injustice can only be overthrown through fighting back. The idea of fighting back is more to preach the postcolonial mindset where talking and writing back to empire is en vogue than the

Marxist ideology of the dialectic clashing. Marley sees the black fight against racism as fighting to regain what belongs to them and to bring back dignity to the *sable* race.

Usually, the idea of fighting violence is evident; it is a kind of violence that Fanon (2004 [1963]) thinks is obvious because white racism has put black people through untold suffering and violent acts. The shootings and killings in South Africa in the 1970s and 1980s, the killings and police racial killings in the United States of America, white racism in all of Europe and even the racial politics that finds itself in sports and football are a few examples to project white racism as unjust and violent. In so doing, Marley becomes a militant black fighter for the restoration of his race all over the world.

The philosophy behind reggae music is the outright attack on the postcolonial leadership characterised by arrogance, incompetence and the mimicry of colonial ideals. Mbembe (1992) is one of the postcolonial scholars who has generally evaluated and theorised on postcolonial power, especially in Africa and the black world. Besides Mbembe's postulation on the binaries that separate the "people" and the "ruler," his description of power as banal in the postcolonial settings is fascinating and requires some keen attention. Mbembe interprets power in postcolonial spaces as a construct that missed its mark, fuelled by the colonial and imperialist zest to stifle the progress of postcolonial societies. In this regard, he focuses on the buffoonery that has characterised "leadership" in Jamaica and the black world in general.

Unfortunately, the frivolity and the meanness of postcolonial "rulership" has become a norm and therefore, hard to interrogate because of repressive institutions and the government policy of economic stagnation and the construction of the nouveau riche class. This build-up only fuels conflict that has characterised regimes in the black world. Mbembe's discourse suggests that power management, as it has been and has been constructed, in much of the postcolony can only lead to violence. He writes as he gives the characteristics of the postcolony in these words, "the postcolony is also made up of a series of corporate institutions and political machinery which, once they are in place, constitute a distinctive regime of violence" (p. 3). It is therefore no gainsaying that much of the conflicts and civil strife that has characterised the postcolonial states have stemmed from poor leadership led by people without any focus and vision for the country. People who are unwilling to learn or listen to the people they rule see the Nation-State as their spoils to plunder.

However, rulers in the black world, for the most part, devise strategies to remain in power and are noted to be rulers who want to rule for life. In most cases, the revolts that come from the "people" have exposed these rulers as people without focus, weak and irresponsible, which Mbembe (1992, p. 4) describes as "zombie leadership." To him, zombification meant "that each [the ruler and the ruled] robbed the other of their vitality and has left them both impotent." Marley's music focuses on this jigsaw between the ruler and the ruled. Interestingly, Marley takes sides with the ruled, which makes him an anti-establishment artist whose dream has almost always been to debunk the hegemonic space that was and has been constructed in Jamaica, the Caribbean and the black world.

Marley entitles one of his songs "Crazy Baldheads." This title shows that the singer/persona is being confrontational with these bald men who, according to the singer/poet are ruining their town. The harmonic and melodic beauty of the song carries the message of a revolution as the singer/persona calls on the people to rebel against their rulers. The central message in the song shows the singer's dissatisfaction with the fact that in a country that may be said to belong to all its citizens, some people – the bald-headed men – are reaping seriously from the labour of the poor. Bond (2006) argues that looting from Africa's [and the Caribbean's] wealth has been a fundamental factor for poverty to become almost permanent and worse still, the attitude of the post-independence leader that has accumulated wealth and cared little about the people. Marley's singer/persona in the song sees the rulers referred to as "crazy baldhead" as people plundering the land where he and the people struggle to build. In this connection, injustice is enshrined by the ruling class. In an angry tone, the singer/persona states,

> I 'n I build a cabin;
> I 'n I plant the corn;
> Didn't my people before me
> Slave for this country?

This question is a profound reminder to the junta that the people contributed not only to the wellbeing of the Nation-State, metaphorically reflected in the song as "town," but are part of the history-making of the States. Indeed, historicism is quickly shifting from the unipolar voice of the victor's history to opening spaces for the history of the vanquished to be told (Trouillot, 1995). Through this song and many other of Marley's music, history is told from the perspective of the oppressed and voiceless people. The singer in these lines reveals that the history of Jamaica from slavery to the present has been built by the people alongside the present rulers. Thus, injustice comes in with the rulers treating the "people" with disdain and look at them "with that scorn, / then you eat up all my corn." One of the catchy techniques that one finds throughout the song is the possessive pronouns and adjectives "I," "my," "we," and "you." These pronouns underscore the "self" and "other" binary; as Marley puts it, none in society is excluded from the blocs. The fact that Jamaica, the Caribbean and the black world are divided by the ruled and ruler binaries as the song reveals, is a significant cause for conflict.

In the song, these pronouns and adjectives strengthen the ideology of "owning," in this case, owning the Nation-State. This fundamental issue in most of the Caribbean and the black world is the fact that Nation-States have strong men and weak institutions. Thus, the paternal image of the rulers is in vogue. In this event, the well-constructed "strong man" is also referred to as the "father of the nation," the "founding father of the nation," whom every other person must accept the place of being his "child." Thus, this "strong man" becomes the owner of the nation. These kinds of rulers have even been described by their acolytes as "creators"; who justified their deifying image to the embarrassment of their listeners. Therefore, the call for the people to take over and chase these rulers out of the land raises the struggle for ownership of the Nation-State. The Nation-State in the song is metonymically represented as "town" and, in some cases like in the last stanza, "yown." The struggle for ownership of the State becomes a severe problem as the different sides of the ideologies in society will always end up in conflict. Fukuyama (1992) illustrates this as he argues that conflict in society has come because of ideologies such that it is common in most societies to get expressions like the Left/Right divide. Again, it further splits to moderate and extreme as the people start questioning the weak Nation-States that strong men construct. As said earlier, these political ideologies include everyone in society because each side of the divide feels and claims ownership of the society. Marley's singer/personae in "Crazy Baldheads" attributes the Nation-State to be that of the people, and here, Marley advocates a strong State: "Chase those crazy baldheads/ Out of our town." Here, the image of chasing connotes violence. The ruling class, as the singer/persona points out, is the problem of the postcolonial society and therefore is no longer needed.

By terming the Jamaican leadership as "crazy baldheads," Marley suggests that male leadership has failed. However, as a patriarch himself, Marley does not open up to avenues of inclusive leadership in the postcolonial Nation-State. This explains why in most, if not all, of his politically conscious songs but for "No, Woman, No Cry," he reveals a paucity of women's action and activism.

However, as the song supposes, chasing the crazy baldheads may just be an opportunity for women to become more assertive in leadership. After all, women's leadership has proven helpful in the postcolony especially after war. In fact, in this song, Marley may well be prescribing a more inclusive leadership of the different people occupying the world he imitates.

CONCLUSION: "ONE LOVE," THE KEY TO CONFLICT RESOLUTION

Marley is also a humanist and a black person with the message of living in peace and love. The soundtrack "One Love" reveals Marley as a humanist of the highest order. Regarding the finesse, no Marley's song is compared to the song. It is a masterpiece from every standard of music and Reggae music in particular. It is one song that Marley builds with harmonic duets and a lead voice that dominate all parts of the song. Such musicality enforces the central theme of the piece, which is love. The celebrating and lamenting tone that overrides the song seems to be one of the rare times that music and lyrics share the same meaning and melody.

In the song, Marley becomes a pastor/priest and a philosopher at the same time. As a pastor/priest, Marley builds his love ideology on theo-principles of love, which to him is the incarnation of God. He sees love as the solution to the world's conflicts. Marley's love is not referring to sentimental emotions. It is the kind of love that Martin Luther King Jr (Washington, 1986) describes as the *Agape* love. To King, *Agape* is understanding, creative, and redemptive goodwill for all men (Washington, 1986). Marley's "One Love" projects love for humankind as a divine and holy process. Such love as King preached and as Marley enforces, is the only way inequality and injustice can stop reigning. Listening to the song, one has the feeling of yearning as both the lead singer and the choric duet wish for "one love" and "one heart." Love, as the singer/personae brings out, is the children's call. The lead voice sings, "Hear the children cry'in' (One Love)/ Hear the children cry'in' (One Heart)" the first melody ends with a fifth and the second melody with the root (tunic). This melodic line that is in itself resolved shows completeness in the children's desire for love. Marley's call for love is appreciated in children's innocence and goodwill and epitomised by Jesus's teaching that heaven is for those who are like children.

To emphasise the call for godly love and human purity, the singer/speaker sees those who orchestrate violence and pain as sinners. "Is there a place for the hopeless sinner/Who has hurt all mankind just to save his own beliefs?" In Marley's philosophy, those at the root of injustice and pain have no place in the Lord (who in the context of the song is a supreme judge) for which he calls on the people to come together and "give thanks to and feel alright." Marley's conclusions are therefore, attractive even though seemingly old-fashioned and primitive to modernist and post-modernist views that peace, love and harmony in the world can come only through the Man. The singer/persona sings, "Let's get together to fight this only Armageddon (one Love)/ So when the *Man* comes there will be no more doom." Marley calls on humanity to unite and fight all sources of evil, division and conflict. And the Man coming to end all doom shows that peace on earth can only come through this man who is to come and that is Jesus Christ.

REFERENCES

Ashcroft, B., Griffiths, G. & Helen Tiffin. (1989). *The empire writes back: Theory and practice in post-colonial literatures.* Routledge.

Bond, P. (2006). *Looting Africa: The economics of exploitation.* Zed Books.

Chevannes, B. (2001). Jamaican diaspora identity: The metaphor of Yaad. In P. Taylor (Ed.). *Religion, identity and cultural difference in the Caribbean* (pp. 129-137). Indiana University Press.

DeLoughrey, E. M. (2007). *Routes and roots: Navigating Caribbean and Pacific island literatures.* University of Hawai'i Press.

Elleke, B. (1994). *Colonial and postcolonial literature: Migrant metaphors.* Oxford University Press.

Fanon, F. (2004). *The wretched of the earth.* (R. Philcox, Trans.) Grove Press.

Forest, R. (1985). Jamaica's rebel music. *A world to win*, 74-85.

Fredrickson, G. M. (2002). *Racism: A short history.* Princeton University Press.

Fukuyama, F. (1992). *The end of history and the last man.* Free Press.

Gilroy, P. (1993). *The black atlantic: Modernity and double consciousness.* Verso.

Guido, B., Bracalenti, R., Braham, P. & Gindro, S. (2003). *Dictionary of race, ethnicity and culture.* SAGE Publications.

Huntington, S. P. (1993). "The clash of civilization". *Foreign Affairs*, 22-49.

Jameson, F. (1997). *Postmodernism, or, the cultural logic of late capitalism.* Duke University Press.

Jeong, H.-W. (2008). *Understanding conflict and conflict analysis.* Sage.

Mayer, B. (2004). *Beyond neutrality: Confronting the crisis in conflict resulution.* Jessy-Bass.

Mbembe, A. (1992). "Provisional notes on the postcolony." *Journal of the International African Institute*, 3-34.

Said, E. (1993). *Culture and imperialism.* Vintage Books.

Said, E. (1996). *Representations of the intellectual.* Vintage Books.

Sandole, D. J. (2007). *Peace Security in the postmodern world: The OSCE and conflict resolution.* Routledge.

Sean, L.-M. (2001). "The Dieasporic mo(ve)ments: Indentureship and Indo-Caribbean identity." In P. Taylor, *Nation dance: Religion, identity and cultural difference in the Caribbean* (pp. 171-192). Indiana University Press.

Stephens, G. (1999). *On racial frontiers: The new culture of Frederick Douglass, Ralph Ellison, and Bob Marley.* Cambridge University Press.

Taylor, C. (1991). *The malaise of modernity.* House of Anansi Press Limited.

Thiong'o, N. W. (1982). *Writers in politics: A re-engagement with issues of literature and society.* Heinemann.

Tizard, B. & Phonix, A. (2002). *Black, white or mixed race? Race and racism in the lives of young people of mixed parentage.* Routledge.

Trouillot, M.-R. (1995). *Silencing the past.* Beacon Press.

Washington, J. M. (1986). *A testimony of hope: The essential writings and speeches of Martin Luther King, jr.* HarperCollins Publishers.

William, L. J. & Brecke, P. (2003). *War and reconciliation: Reason and emotion in conflict resolution.* The MIT Press.

3

Spatial Transcendence and the (Re)Invention of Space in James Joyce's *A Portrait of the Artist as a Young Man*

MBUH TENNU MBUH

INTRODUCTION: SPATIALITY FROM LEVINAS TO JOYCE

If modernism scrutinised traditional borderlines and opted for more impalpable zones of existence, it was because the "traditional" world had become a contested site in the wake of new intellectual and artistic insights in the imagination of the West. The Empire had collapsed, the Commonwealth of Nations was grappling anew for universal conquest, and, ironically, the United Kingdom's closest neighbour, Ireland, challenged the realisation of these dreams by staying out of the bloc. The fact that one of the greatest writers of the twentieth century, James Joyce, hailed from Ireland and struggled in both his life and writing to be reconciled with his Anglo-Irish identity proves the delicate nature of colonial boundary formations and their implications into the twenty-first century. In discussing the notion of borders and the spaces they demarcate in Joyce's *A Portrait*, this chapter argues that the novel imagines new spaces and identities by overriding previous linear or binary constructs and replaces them with concentric variants from the bolting imagination of the hero. At the same time, it is apparent that in creating a hero who seeks newer frontiers with only a vague hope and promise to return, Joyce sacrificed the physical space of nationalist passions for the virtual alternative of the escapist exile, obviously seduced by a modernist advocacy. This ambivalence makes *A Portrait* counter-productive to the nationalist agenda of ascertaining space and borders and ironically enhances the neutralisation of borders, which colonialism nurtured.

Critics continue to privilege modernist characteristics in James Joyce, whose books, as the preface to Attridge's (2000, p. xiii) representative *Joyce Effects* reminds us, "go off like inventive and spectacular fireworks, and one response is to sit back and enjoy them—enjoy their intricate construction, their subtle phrasings, their play with conventions and expectations, their engagement with the twists and turns of history, their often hilarious exposure of prejudice and pomposity." If, however, "the twists and turns of history" are assessed from a critical frame that was more intimate to Joyce's overall worries with his place in Irish history, whether in anticipation or from hindsight, it will be obvious that we are dealing with parallel visions from the same lens. The stylistic emphasis on how "[w]ords fall apart before his eyes, disintegrating into the primeval chaos of their elements" (Ellmann 2010, p. 130) overwrites the historical concern from which this innovation is bred.

Levinas (1989, p. 49) adopted a feminist approach in elaborating on "[t]he feminine in existence [as] an event different from that of spatial transcendence"— which has since been further elaborated upon as "the parental mode of being" that defines paternity, (Marcus 2008, p. 145); or as "the intimate other of the dwelling and eroticism, who does not speak, and who seems, at least within the erotic, barely distinguishable from the 'there is'" (Large, 2015, p. 125). However, my intention is to explore its applicability in a nationalist context within which spatiality and transcendence oppose an abstract or gendered otherness beyond the borders of textual intelligibility, in Joyce, in which case, the transcendence of space is connected to both colonial exploration and the maintenance of its resultant status-quo. In Joyce's modernist aesthetics, textual boundaries (re)invent their own essences and consequently, the experimentation for which he and his peers were so famous attributes meaning that may be contested through the very solution it offers, especially when we engage the textual landscape from a postcolonial perspective that derides the narcissism of modernists. More relevantly, Levinas (1999, p. 44) asserts that "[t]he movement toward the ultimate totality, an absolute world or being, admits of differences, even in its formalism. The totality of individuals belonging to the same genus differs from the totality of men belonging to a nation, which in turn is different from the totality of episodes making up a story, from that of the points making up a space." In *A Portrait*, Stephen Dedalus is obsessed with the juxtaposition of his identity, in generic terms, with its location within a national space. In his attempt to reconcile these poles, he begins to speculate beyond the national space while simultaneously creating a parallel space within the text. Ultimately, he struggles to convince us that textual space can be privileged over material space. In acknowledging "difference," Dedalus is also caught in a purist illusion and accommodates the Other only as far as it does not destabilise his centrality. In this case, the author and his character suffer from an alien consciousness that only uproots them as they struggle to affirm their sense of Self. Joyce's (and by implication, Stephen's) exclusive nationalism instead reinforces the complications of decolonisation, which Irish nationalists struggled to dismantle.

To understand Stephen's role in (mis)appropriating space in postcolonial Ireland, it is essential to remember that his failure is that of a child who not only forgets but rejects the folklore of his people and goes on to invent a contested alternative. Therefore, the imperative of when and how the child never forgets becomes cardinal to an understanding of how Joyce's modernist experimentation scarred the postcolonial expectations of his character. Mrs Ramsay's famous reflection in Woolf's (1999, p. 85) *To the Lighthouse* (when she covertly indicts her husband's blunt response against their son's hopes) that "children never forget" is not only significant in how she and Joyce rationalised the child archetype in their search for and affirmation of modernist aesthetics to postwar uncertainties in the West but also in the possible mapping of the world around us through a child's cognitive reactions. Fear of the outcome leads to euphemistic usages by adults. It explains why the child is key to the notion of salvation and also why colonial authority mirrored colonised demographics through the child's psyche. The troubling possibility of the child (never) forgetting helps us to discern the further challenge posed by the child's psychology as it evolves within a nationalist matrix. Stephen Dedalus is not the typical child of the colonial imagination, and almost every sentence in the novel testifies to this "difference." He is sensitive to a fault, and when interdicted about the liberties of his imagination, he resorts to an even more frightening strategy of internalising his thoughts and thus becomes unpredictable to the authoritative superstructure. Such anonymity, which is vital to his reliance on memory as a reconstructive medium in the much-needed cultural renaissance for Ireland, eventually verbalises his "silence" into "cunning" as an indicator of his representative recalcitrance and then transforms that "silence" into a personalised nationalist weapon of protest. However, to achieve this, he transforms into a rejectionist whose memory serves only as a symbolic lore in the imagined space of exile. His own growing rationalisation of meaning as evolving from his subjective psyche thus challenges his credentials as an alternative to the Irish nationalists whom he despises.

At the start of the novel, Stephen's childhood imagination conceives of Ireland as a constraining space; his fantasies are as dreamy as they are unable to be restrained, and caught in adult rationalism of Irishness around him, he struggles throughout the novel to define space as a complement to identity. National politics is played out in the domestic environment of conflicting and compromising sentiments. What Joyce projects onto Stephen's consciousness is the distorted configuration of Ireland through the dominant ideologies of religion and politics. The very partisan nature of these ideologies is both the result of foreign, precisely English, domination and nationalists' attempts to resist such force. Underlying such tensions is the failure to properly analyse Joyce's Ireland along its colonial trajectory of perceived and unperceived motivations. As in every colonial situation, the English never privileged indigenous values but instead concentrated on formatting native space into the alien mentality. Ironically, even by the time of Joyce, Irish nationalism still adopted sentimental reactions against English dominance; and, but for the blunt realism of representative writers like J.M. Synge and the later Yeats, the whole project of Irish identity would have anticipated what was to follow in anti-colonial agitations in Africa - a compromised neo-colonialism.

Against this background, Joyce presents his character, at once self-reflexive and experimental, whose desire for self-knowledge is also the fate of Ireland. The fairyland space of baby Stephen's imagination represents what he will strive to overcome and again anticipates—because he cannot be accommodated by the hypocrisy of institutionalised notions of right or wrong—the abstract world of exile into which he will escape finally. Intimidated by his mother and Dante for expressing innocent matrimonial desires toward Eileen, he seeks refuge under the table, which metamorphoses into the conventional exilic space at the novel's end. Having failed to be inspired by an organic Irish past, beyond the angry references to Irish heroes and their inability (according to him) to rescue the land, Stephen, like Joyce, does not understand the land which he hopes to celebrate and protect. Joyce's inability to belong to any modernist group, "always suspicious of groups and fought hard to maintain his artistic independence" (Bulson, 2006, p. 19), indicates a conceited mentality that was as exclusive as his professed revisionism is idealistic. His was an intellectual engagement with Ireland through modernist shades of aesthetic meaning without a *lived* history in need of rewriting that space both for himself and his character(s).

JOYCE'S HISTORICISATION OF IRELAND

The discourse of Ireland has always been contentious, probably because, like every *small* territory in the vicinity of an expansionist neighbour, the quest for identity depends to a large extent on the dynamics of dominance and resistance. Empathising with such a space requires significant knowledge of its evolution, which should complement the ideological formations that have characterised its state. The Ireland about which Joyce wrote had been transformed through the incursion of alien religious ritual, demonised through colonial domination, while attempts to rehabilitate it were mostly rendered through revivalists who adopted a sentimental nationalism. The causality between the two is reactionary and accounts for why a writer like Synge became such a controversial figure through his mood of enacting a realistic social drama that dispenses with the nationalist gloss. Joyce does not seem to fit into any of these categories, and his work becomes another intellectual attempt to rationalise Irish identity from the margins.

The variant of Irish history he proposes is vetted mainly by his own biases. Little wonder then that "Joyce's most influential readers can disclose nothing but polar opposition between Joycean modernism and Irish nationalism," arguing that "his explorations of language, personal identity and history are simply incompatible with the reverence displayed for tradition and community in nationalist ideology" (Nolan, 1995, p. xi). This reaction can be explained by Joyce's faith in the fact, as expressed in one of his letters, that he was "composing [his] chapter of moral history" in the hope of "tak[ing] the first step towards the spiritual liberation of [his] country" (Dettmar 2004, p. xx). In *Ulysses* Dedalus declares that history is "a nightmare from which I am trying to awake" (Joyce, 2000, p. 42)—with the painful realisation that "he must do so in a language conditioned by that very history" (Dettmar, 2004, p. xxv); while Attridge (2000, p. 78) relates this remark to "the Ulyssean episode for which, according to Joyce's schema for the book, history is the designated art." Through his metaphorical approach to history, we see Stephen in *A Portrait* distancing himself from the stereotype while struggling intellectually to activate an alternative. Reducing (the study of) history to "those [great] men and what they did" (Joyce, 1969, p. 47), Stephen erroneously envisages his participation in it from the *scholarly* rationalisation of such accounts and not from the indigenous and culturally relevant context of Ireland. When he philosophises on the fact that "[t]his race and this country and this life produced me" and that "I shall express myself as I am" (Joyce, 1969, p. 188), the embodied totality does not cohere with the cultural field for the "produced" consciousness; rather, we see him already initiating the process of distancing himself from the familiar lore of his people in order to establish the necessary intellectual alibi for *his* "difference." It should however be pointed out that a postcolonial historical narrative is averse, implicitly, to its conceptualisation into modernist-structuralist options, and as Dettmar (2004, p. xxvi) notes, Stephen's reaction to English words "[owes] to the history of colonial subjection of Ireland by Great Britain." Significantly, he points out how Joyce's work "seem[s] to imply that all versions of history are made in language and are, by virtue of that fact, ideological constructions, weavings and reweavings of old stories, fusions of stock character types, blendings of different national languages, dialects, and registers" (Dettmar, 2004, p. 80). This is an important clue to a possible vindication of the modernist author, only that his subject matter still restricts his freedom of theoretical choice, especially when he fails to appropriate the colonial language (meant to shed light on that subject) like a postcolonial writer and instead "refines" it into modernist sophistication.

Scholars are generally unanimous on the fact that the distortion of history is a vital device for prefiguring colonial hegemony. Pellin (2003, p. 1) has suggested as much in his analysis of the mistrust that characterises Anglo-Irish relations by pointing out that "[w]hat particularly makes the history [of these relations] so difficult is the fact that far too many historians have used the writing of history as a means of perpetuating the conflict they purport to delineate." On the literary side of this argument, Nash (2006, p. 30) identifies in Joyce a desire to "seek historical accuracy" in the further ambivalence at the end of *A Portrait* to "encounter for the millionth time [with] the reality of experience"; and which for Nash is a pattern that inspires a "monotony [that] might yet lead to the 'forging' of something as yet Uncreated." Nash's attempt to vindicate Joyce's exilic propaganda as "a particularly apt condition since the exile, by virtue of his having left, knows that at least this singular event is possible," suggests a speculative historicity that can easily falsify the very slate of history into personal subjectivities. This is more so the case when History is homogenised "as ground and untranscendable horizon [that] needs no particular theoretical justification" (Jameson, 1981, p. 102), thus rendering it as another new historicist concession for which those whose past was compromised are expected to be grateful.

The distorted history that Irish writers and historians draw on relates to what is represented in Anglo-history and literature as Ireland often colludes alien as indigenous codes. According to Kilberd (1996, p. 9), "If Ireland had never existed, the English would have invented it." Buoyed by his modernist and Oxbridge peers, Joyce evidently exploited this functional attribute of colonial civilisation for his aesthetic purpose. Again, in *The Irish Writer and the World*, Kilberd (2005, pp. 1 & 3) elaborates on this possibility by emphasising the exilic status of the typical Irish writer and how it determined and affected his or her writing: "The problem faced by many [diasporic Irish writers] was the discovery that an 'image' had preceded them to their first overseas encounter."

This imaging of Ireland was therefore prejudicial and influenced the writers in a way that simplified the notion of space into a subjective category of the soul in which "[m]any narrow-gauge Irish nationalists ... patent[ed] an Ireland that was less a truly liberated zone than a sort of not-England, in which every virtue of the colonising country had its equal but opposite Irish counterpart."

The opening sentence of *A Portrait* thus speculates on the (re)invention of space (depending on whose perspective is considered) as a variable of traditional temporality in folktales. Like every mythical "beginning" in which fathomless time is arrested into a formal structure whose meaning then prescribes what follows in contemporary life, the "once-upon-a-time" background to Joyce's narrative approximates an idyllic past — "a very good time it was"—from which the present and the future may be ascertained in superlatives of cultural pride. But this is as far as the good times go for both the individual and community in Joyce, first because concentrating on such historicity demands the use of a traditional style in which its aesthetics are couched and second because the fairyland setting of the child's imagination in which humans and animals blend—evoking a pastoral paradise—is corrupted by contemporary pressures and their respective biases. Juxtaposed space at the beginning is already a contested paradigm, and Stephen's consciousness throughout the novel will have to confront its changing shades in artistic and nationalist terms. Such an engagement, which revaluates traditional patterns of identity, belonging, and loyalty, also relates to perceptions of the controlling authority by its subordinated alternative. In other words, conservative and liberal forces are at work here over the occupation and use of space. Levinas' suggestion that space may be used in gendered ways reinforces the argument that in Joyce's novel, the colonial imagination assumes a phallic disposition to prescribe and attribute meaning. In other words, Joyce's Ireland is feminised with all the attributes of invisibility, which Stephen is positioned to challenge. In doing this, he relates to existing spaces in confrontational ways but also imagines or invents new spaces that shift the debate about Irish nationalism into an alternative to the fairy context, that of exile. How such a situation develops can be understood from Levinas's association of conquering and conquered territories with male-female potentials of othered presence. Toward the end of the novel, Stephen speculates on success as an illusion of exile, which, in fact implies spacelessness: "I do not fear to be alone or to be spurned for another or to leave whatever I have to leave. And I am not afraid to make a mistake, even a great mistake, a life-long mistake, and perhaps as long as eternity too" (Joyce, 1969, p. 229). This, at best, is the indeterminate context of exile in which

Stephen's hope is rooted in his (re)historicisation illusion.

RELIGIOUS SPATIALITY OF *A PORTRAIT*

In the novel, religious tensions provide the arena for bitter confrontation between Roman Catholics and Protestants. Dogmatic definitions conflict with the assertion of space as both a spiritual and physical realm, reminiscent of how the Christian ideology of the Anglo-Saxon world perturbed indigenous ritual during the Dark Ages. Stephen is the modernist personification of these tensions, now assuming more militant poses. Stephen seems to be engaged in the reconfiguration of a religious mode in which a personal God can substitute what he considers to be an adulterated archetype. Here, his reliance on personal mythology derives from his knowledge of other mythologies, now almost obsolete or questionable, such as Christian and Greek versions, with which he is identified. An embodiment of the Christian martyr and the Greek artist implies a need to subvert their respective uniqueness and offers the hero a licence for recalcitrant dismemberment of the conventional vision. But while both Stephen and Dedalus celebrate the fact of their heroism within the mythological and transcendental contexts of their respective calling, Stephen has the arduous task of situating himself within a space which he simultaneously courts and rejects. Within this space, God is either dead or the approach to his abode is complicated by ideological rivalries, orchestrating a punitive pedagogy. One example of religious dissent in the novel relates to Stephen's attitude to perceived injustice. When he is unfairly beaten by the prefect of studies, the "low dark narrow corridor that led through the castle to the rector's room" (Joyce, 1969, p. 47) and through which he walks to report the disciplinarian, reflect the nebulous national space as hellish. This passage exemplifies what Frye (2000, pp. 139 & 147) ascribes to one component of a binary in his mythological study, "which takes the form of two contrasting worlds of total metaphorical identification, one desirable and the other undesirable." The latter is a "demonic human world" which is "held together by a kind of molecular tension of egos, a loyalty to the group or the leader which diminishes the individual, or, at best, contrasts his pleasure with his duty or honour." Even the religious quarrels at home and how they generate complementary barriers at the political level are all signs and extensions of the collapsed moral authority of institutionalised religion.

In the novel, Dante personifies fundamentalist Roman Catholicism, and her extreme fervour affects family unity. Stephen's earlier passion for Eileen is doomed by this anarchical disposition on Dante's part, when "she did not like him [Stephen] to play with Eileen because Eileen was a protestant" (Joyce, 1969, p. 30). If Dante's opposition stems from a childhood memory of how protestant kids "used to make fun of the litany of the Blessed Virgin," it indicates the extent to which successive generations of Irish are caught up in the religious tensions that are external to their national identity. As Stephen will realise at the height of his recalcitrance, such tension is staged and accepted by both colonising and colonised mentalities, respectively, to justify the one's contested presence and the other's perennial blame strategy. What he fails to realise—and the failure will define his exilic declarations—is the fact that Dublin, which he hates so passionately, is a victim of grafted English identity, and the anti-colonial struggle of the citizens becomes a necessary momentum for change, which Joyce's contemporaries like Synge and Yeats finally affirmed in more militant ways.

Again, an indication of this unique approach is evident in his prayer: he does not submit to God conventionally but rather places himself in a relatively authoritative position in which he seems to succumb only because he expects God to grant his will unconditionally. In archetypal terms, he already betrays the arrogant self-will which propels Icarus to his demise. If we compare Stephen's prayer to its formal version when he is asked to pray at table, the formative nature of his ideological rebellion will be evident: "Bless us, O Lord, and these Thy gifts which through Thy bounty we are about to receive through Christ our Lord. Amen" (Joyce, 1969, p. 24). The mechanical nature of prayer here does not appeal to his personalisation of ideology, and in preparing himself for an Icarus-type rebellion against the authoritative forces that surround him, Stephen ignores physical, historical, and cultural spaces within which political and religious atrocities collude with English imperialism to redefine that space and the people's priorities. What is privileged is his very personal space, which is so personalised as the antithesis of what he sees as a corrupt and violated space. By insisting on exploring his own subjective universe, Stephen also violates the ideals of Irish nationalists and their collective, if at times contestable, approach to independence.

What then follows in chapters two and three is Stephen's struggles against the systemic flaws, as he sees them, of conditioning the rebellious individual to their ideals. When he reflects on "the question of honour," for instance, he concludes that it was "trivial to him":

> While his mind had been pursuing its intangible phantoms and turning in irresolution from such pursuit he had heard about him the constant voices of his father and of his masters, urging him to be a gentleman above all things

and urging him to be a good catholic above all things. These voices had now come to be hollow sounding in his ears. When the gymnasium had been opened he had heard another voice urging him to be strong and manly and healthy and when the movement towards national revival had begun to be felt in the college yet another had bidden him to be true to his country and help to raise up her language and tradition (*Portrait* 75).

So burdened by this din of voices, including those of "his school comrades [which] urged him to be a decent fellow, to shield others from blame or to beg them off and to do his best to get free days for the school," Stephen sees his leadership potentials as already compromised by frivolous expectations that do not reflect the nationalist agenda. This clash of voices, which he confronts, is part of what Stephen dreads as a false and falsifying vision of the world he is expected to prop up. In rejecting such distracting militancy, Stephen simultaneously seeks his happiness "only when he was far from them, beyond their call, alone or in the company of phantasmal comrades" (Joyce, 1969, p. 73). This tendency of rejecting what is physical and palpable in preference for its mental variant reduces his project of a new Ireland into precisely what he rejects, the exile's dream rendered as only phantasmal. When he distances himself from the secular and religious institutions which condition his consciousness or attempts to do so, Stephen also denies himself the possibility of learning even from the cultural mistakes committed by his forebear. The child in him remembers only select bits of Irish lore, which are then compromised by modernist agnosticism.

POLITICAL SPACE AND THE PROBLEM OF BEING AN ARTIST

The independence of the Republic of Ireland in 1922 was only a part victory for nationalists because the Northern Ireland question remained unresolved. As such, the Ireland which Joyce wrote about is still undergoing the throes of colonialism because of sectarian sentiments that overlap with devolutionary politics from Number 10 Downing Street. The ambivalence, which characterises Stephen's embodied identification for or against nationalist expectations stretches his potential and commitment in a way that casts doubt on his intellectual and nationalist personalities. Given the hostile interaction between religion and politics, it is possible to suggest that Stephen is most confused about whether or not to serve God or Caesar and in what way(s). On the one hand, he addresses the Irish Question from an escapist mental zone in much the same way as Yeats had sentimentalised it at the height of his obsession for Maud Gonne while claiming a nationalist vision that cannot be realised within the very space that he condemns.

Parnell is the controversial political and cultural link in Stephen's mediation of the tension between England and Ireland. Significantly, Stephen is attentive whenever "his elders spoke constantly of the subjects nearer their hearts, of Irish politics, of Munster and of the legends of their own family." And having "glimpses of the real world" through such interactions, Stephen also realises that "[t]he hour when he too would take part in the life of that world seemed drawing near and in secret he began to make ready for the great part which he felt awaited him" (Joyce, 1969, p. 55). How he responds to the challenge and expectation eventually is conditioned by his experiences of the tense relationship between his family members, his subjective evaluation of the political situation, and how ultimately, politics itself becomes a tasteless engagement for him.

Stephen's nationalist narrative is derailed by a preference that restricts him to the fairy world from which Yeats eventually escaped, therefore acknowledging what Irish revivalists had criticised as unpatriotic in Synge. Writing postcolonial Ireland, Stephen's vacillation between using art as a nationalist platform for universal humanity and modernist demands for aesthetic beauty betrays his limited commitment to art as a viable weapon of change. In this way, the other worlds discussed above are subsumed into the artistic, where Eileen, for instance, is transformed into Mercedes and ultimately rarefied into the apparition of ultimate beauty from the river. The beauty of the beginning, which he desired and ran into trouble with his mother and Dante, as a result, has been perfected into an invisible personality, only affirmed by the senses, with no practical influence on the cause he is expected to defend. The shift from the substantial to a spectral personality corresponds to Stephen's symbolic abandonment of the Irish cause.

Space is therefore both defined and limited for Stephen as variations of artistic possibility and not of the nationalist's realism. His growth and maturity correspond to attempts to understand the definitions implicated in his personal development. His poem is an early indication of this rationalisation of space and growth in it. Stephen realises that both education and religion offer liberation strategies which, as he realises painfully, fail to be fulfilling. The failure results from the fact that the two reflect colonial strategies of control, but since Stephen is not really a "people's" nationalist, at least not as defined by his peers and compatriots, he then relates to them with personal recalcitrance that does not recognise the collective vision.

The physical worlds of the novel become increasingly disgusting and alienating, represented by Dublin as "a maze of narrow and dirty lanes" (Joyce, 1969, p. 91). From this, the educational and religious environments are implicated in the conscripting design for the erstwhile militant-artist. For Stephen, the child, geographical awareness (as we have seen) evolves from a fairy setting through Dante's vested intelligence to his own attempt to define *his* world beyond the normative. Regarded by Stephen as someone who "knew a lot of things," Dante "[teaches] him where the Mozambique Channel was and what was the longest river in America and what was the name of the highest mountain in the moon" (Joyce, 1969, pp. 11-12). Dante's pedagogy, like that of Father Arnall (who "knew more than Dante because he was a priest"), deals with prescribed universals within which the representative places of Stephen's academic adventure become "authorised" versions and not meant to be questioned. Thus, Stephen's growing curiosity is meant to be conditioned by this apparently superior reasoning. This already poses a problem for a character whose curiosity is rooted in origins and the meanings that derive from these.

Writing himself, so to speak, Stephen is simultaneously defining—or attempting to define—the cultural space of his composite interactions. Formal geography lessons are abstract and peripheral to his concern. His reluctance or inability to "learn the names of places in America" results from the fact that "they were all different places with different names. They were all in different countries, and the countries were in continents, and the continents were in the world and the world was in the universe" (Joyce, 1969, p. 11). This basic orientation in geography focuses on the general at the expense of the particular, but Stephen is already anticipating a postcolonial concern with place and identity, a challenge to the arrogation and renaming of indigenous space by colonial authority. Breaking away from what is obviously a blueprint for colonial education, Stephen "turn[s] to the flyleaf of the geography and read[s] what he had written there":

> Stephen Dedalus
> Class of Elements
> Clongowes Wood College
> Sallins
> County Kildare
> Ireland
> Europe
> The World
> The Universe (Joyce, 1969, p. 11)

Such inverse reading privileges the Self not as a mere binary complement of colonial assumptions which thrive on the fortunes of the Other, but as the very location for the problematisation of the polarised binary. In postcolonial jargon, Stephen challenges the centrality of the colonial mindset by creating a new centre for his representative Self. Significantly, he views his writing as "himself, his name and where he was," a denial of colonial othering. It is a reminder that the site for self-knowledge is self-defined; the quest for meaning also becomes the means to (or from) such self-definition and self-realisation. Stephen's pride, even at this tender age ("[t]hat was in his writing"), can be understood when his writing is compared with the version by his friend, Fleming:

> Stephen Dedalus is my name,
> Ireland is my nation.
> Clongowes is my dwelling place
> And heaven my expectation.

Already, there is both a stylistic and thematic divergence here: Stephen's connotative version is abstract poetry in the modernist style in which meaning is only suggested and not overtly stated; the chosen medium, even in its oral form, from which all other forms of human articulation develop, at least in a creative sense, will complement the written form. On the other hand, Fleming adopts a prosaic style, relies on formal punctuation and rhyme scheme for a sense of traditional "beauty" in poetry, while the themes which he highlights, both earthly and transcendental, are the goal of the type of education which Stephen rejects. Given the sense in which Stephen is becoming aware, a "dwelling place" is the conditioned acceptance of colonial boundaries with which the indigenes should not be concerned because of heavenly expectations. Within the context of Stephen's eventual rebellion, we see how Christianity colluded with the coloniser to appease the colonised with a notion of space that was no longer restricted to anti-colonial demands.

Even more dramatic than Stephen's attempt to personalise space is his imagination of a *beyond* that was antithetical to the Christian dogma of the transcendental. Beyond the vague abstractions of God and heaven, which Christianity celebrates as the ultimate goal of every believer, Stephen's critical appraisal of his flyleaf iconoclasm leads to ontological worries that are again resolved through acknowledgement of his centrality in the scheme: "That was he," and after which he becomes philosophical: "What was after the universe? … [W]as there anything round the universe to show where it stopped before the nothing place began? It could not be a wall; but there could be a thin thin line there all round everything" (Joyce, 1969, p. 12). This limited example of the concentric notion of space in authoritative geography reflects modernist speculations and is no longer defined in traditional binaries. And interestingly, Stephen was imagining in the early decades of the twentieth century what is in vogue today in scientific explorations. For instance, in concluding his foreword to *Exploration of the Outer Heliosphere and the Local Interstellar Medium* (Fisk, 2004, p. vii), whose aim was to probe into the farthest possible reaches beyond the solar system, Lennard A. Fisk, Chair, Space Studies Board, expresses the hope that the "journey will be one of the great explorations of humankind, when we leave the safety of our solar system and venture forth into interstellar space." A close reading of *A Portrait* depicts Stephen's insecurity within his immediate environment in terms of the landscape, his acquaintances, and the ideologies that they propagate. However, his ultimate aim at the end of the novel is not exploratory in order to reinforce his ability to check what threatens him but vagrant speculation after an ideal that has been intellectualised beyond its communal relevance.

The older Stephen gets, therefore, the more he withdraws from the places to which his consciousness is connected. His commitment is "refined" (like the ideal image of the artist within *his* text, which he longs to become), out of physical space/presence into a symbolic space of text and exile. Little wonder then that when his father's friends "made him admit that the Lee was a much finer river than the Liffey" (Joyce, 1969, p. 85), Stephen's reluctance to be so engaged speaks to his aloofness from the militant politics of place and identity. The two rivers, especially the Liffey, inspired Joyce a lot not only in *A Portrait*, but also in *Finnegans Wake* and *Ulysses*. The inspiration was almost prophetic because a James Joyce Bridge was constructed in 2003 to span the Lee. As such, the geography "lesson" in Stephen's imposed pedagogy replicates his struggle with "the censorious memory of his childhood": "He tried to call forth some of its vivid moments but could not. He recalled only names. Dante, Parnell, Clane, Clongowes. A little boy had been taught geography by an old woman who kept two brushes in her wardrobe. Then he had been sent away from home to a college…" (Joyce, 1969, p. 84). His departure from home corresponds to a flitting interest in the immediate concerns of his people, evident in his inability to recollect the intimately "vivid moments" of childhood. In leaving home, also, Stephen begins to shed his innocence, which reflects the naturalism of Ireland, and his growing experience becomes questionable with the expanding sphere of his observation. In this way, he increasingly privileges his own sentiments to the extent that he confuses them with those of the community and in fact, lives with the illusion that his are more authentic.

QUESTIONABLE LANGUAGE OF THE INTELLECTUAL NATIONALIST

Linguistically, Stephen's nationalism is contestable when he condescends on the Irish in preference for the colonising language, English. Concerned with "traces of Cork accent in his speech" (Joyce, 1969, p. 85), Stephen indulges in the use of Latin expressions as a mark of difference, complementing his English. When one of his father's binge-drinking partners "asked him whether it was correct to say: *Tempora mutantur nos et mutamur in illis* or *Tempora mutantur et nos mutamur in illis*" (Joyce, 1969, p. 85), Stephen does not readily disclose his answer, concerned more with his growing dissatisfaction over his father's irresponsible lifestyle and his determination to be different. He only seems to agree with the translated Latin text that "the times change and we change with them." A significant aspect of nationalism, language is being manipulated by Stephen to attain a status that takes him out of the struggle to regain and authenticate both language itself and territory. Latin is the archetypal medium for colonial authority, and to have an affirmative bias for it suggests a less than casual attention to the indigenous voice. As an indicator of his confusion, even as he takes "gradual command ... of language" and "learns to make words belong to him by personalising the definitions" (Bulson, 2006, p. 53), Joyce ironically "associated the attempts of critics to 'delimit his experiments with the English language' with the 'English' attempt to 'set a limit to the march of his nation'" (Nash, 2006, p. 159). To be concerned with the national momentum is one thing; to enhance it accordingly is another. This is so because if, indeed, "language is not one thing with one origin or one function" (Attridge 2000, p. xvii), then we need to know how its functioning can draw hugely on alien experiences in lieu of the native. Stephen's rejection of Irish failed to anticipate a form of linguistic nationalism in Ireland today, evident in "[p]articular concentrations of habitual Irish speakers ... in the main cities of the Republic of Ireland, including Dublin, Cork, Galway, Limerick and Waterford" (O'Rourke, 2011, p. 106).

When his father accompanies him to the bank to cash "the moneys of his exhibition and essay prize," the symbolism of the environment does not impress Stephen. The fact that "his orders [are] on the governor of the bank of Ireland," together with his father's reluctance to leave once the transaction is over, should remind Stephen of the struggle for Irish independence. While he "urge[s] him [his father] to come out," it is the older man who reminds Stephen "that they were standing in the house of commons of the old Irish parliament" (which had been "made obsolete by the Act of Union in 1800"). Mr Dedalus' emotional outburst ("God help us! ... to think of the men of those times, Stephen, Hely Hutchinson and Flood and Henry Grattan and Charles Kendal Bushe, and the noblemen we have now, leaders of the Irish people at home and abroad") is a tribute to 18th-century members of the Irish Parliament known for their oratorical skills"—as Dettmar's footnote to this section explains (Joyce, 1969, p. 85).

Stephen's withdrawal from the collective memory of his national community logically conjures a personal community of his intellectualised soul from which he begins a condescending discourse on everything but Irish nationalism, which he disparages as a failed or betrayed cause. His eventual preference "to be alone with his soul" is also a desire to abandon "a region of viscid gloom" that is reminiscent of the maze over Dublin. Stephen is thus an ambiguous nationalist who discriminates against Englishness at the same time that he is seduced by and implicated in its supremacist ethos. Apart from the sentiments which he recalls as a child over the death of Parnell, Stephen hardly refers to him and other nationalists as patriots whose vision he hopes to emulate or rehabilitate. Instead, he sees his vision as superior to the rest, and it is this supremacist verve in his thought pattern that will raise questions about the functional purpose of what he offers. His repeated reference to Irish nationalists is at best referential, a tactical intellectual-modernist obscurantism that instead highlights his singularity to the extent that he appropriates some of his friends' real-life situations to himself. When he refers to one of the nationalists, Wolfe Tone, in whose memory "a street slab was set," Stephen "remember[s] with bitterness that scene of tawdry tribute" (Joyce, 1969, p. 170). The reason for his anger becomes clearer as we get deeper into the text, and relates to a general sense, for him, of betrayal by Irish informers. At a personal level, his anger—bearing in mind that his father is an ardent Parnellist—is a consequence of the "prolonged ... moment of discouraged poverty" provoked in him by the young girl selling flowers which Stephen is unable to buy. Yet, and unlike his contemporaries, he is unable to craft a more dignifying compliment; and even when the reflection on the tribute to Tone ends with the inscribed words, "Vive l'Irlande," Stephen does not elaborate on the link between French and Irish independence struggle.[11]

---

1   See Pelling's analysis of the effects of the French Revolution, for instance, on Irish

It is this ambivalent attitude—related to the suggestive technique of modernism which Joyce partly fathered—that makes one of his friends, Davin, to question his sense of patriotism: "I can't understand you ... One time I hear you talk against English literature. Now you talk against Irish informers. What with your name and your ideas ... Are you Irish at all?" (Joyce, 1969, p. 187). This is perhaps the most incisive critique of Stephen's eloquence in the novel in terms of his position vis-à-vis the Irish Question and evidence that even Joyce had his moments of self-doubt. "Writing" against the current of colonial authority and expected to be committed toward his dispossessed constituency, Stephen gives the impression that objectivity in his art is enough. As Davin suggests, his very name betrays his militancy because it instead acknowledges Christian and Greek traditions that are significantly responsible for the condition of Ireland and then for Stephen's conceited outlook. Even when Stephen boasts of his family tree in "the office of arms," his friend is not convinced and instead urges him to "be one of us" by becoming more interested in what Davin considers as identity markers: "Why don't you learn Irish? Why did you drop out of the league class after the first lesson?" (Joyce, 1969, p. 187). As a means to "cultural and separatist nationalism" for Ireland (Jackson 2004, p. 138), the League could not give Stephen the uniqueness he desired.

Cornered as such, Stephen again becomes philosophical in defence: "This race and this country and this life produced me ... I shall express myself as I am" (Joyce, 1969, p. 188). What he is, actually, is a hybrid personality, like every postcolonial subject, but unable to see the connection with what he condemns in his race and country. And to justify his own perversity, Stephen instead attributes blame, in self-vindication: "My ancestors threw off their language and took another ... They allowed a handful of foreigners to subject them. Do you fancy I am going to pay in my own life and person debts they made? What for?" (Joyce, 1969, p. 188). There is a fundamental contradiction here—which positions Joyce and his character as two of Jackson's (2004, p. 123) "Irish people [who] were simultaneously major participants in Empire, and a significant source of subversion"—that exposes Stephen's patriotic fervour, when we consider his unworded response to the Dean of Studies' response to his use of Irish:

> The language in which we are speaking is his before it is mine. How different are the words home, Christ, ale, master, on his lips and on mine! I cannot speak or write these words without unrest of spirit. His language, so familiar

---

independence.

and so foreign, will always be for me an acquired speech. I have not made or accepted its words. My voice holds them at bay. My soul frets in the shadow of his language (Joyce, 1969, p. 175).

There is a double-standard here that is typical of the duplicity which undercuts Stephen's affirmation of identity. No wonder that Northrop Frye sees Joyce (positively, unlike our position here) as the sustainer of the "tradition of verbal exuberance" whose "golden age in English literature" was characterised by "expressions of a creative exuberance of which the most typical and obvious sign is the verbal tempest, the tremendous outpouring of words in catalogues, abusive epithets and erudite technicalities" (Frye 2000, p. 236). This modernist tendency compromises indigenous sympathies with language and makes *A Portrait* to vacillate between moods of acceptance and denial.

Apart from over-simplifying the complicated mesh of personalities and the general seductiveness that camouflages the brutality of ideologies that accompany colonial confrontation with his well-trimmed phrase of "a handful of foreigners," Stephen's irresponsibility puts to question his own creative purpose, if his life and art cannot be remedial to the apparent ancestral compromise. Accusing his ancestors of surrendering their linguistic identity for another's, Stephen can be imagined in exile doing just what Joyce did in Trieste, where he learned Triestino, "a living language that he would continue to speak with his two children, Giorgio and Lucia, for the rest of his life" (Bulson, 2006, p. 7). His stance may be justified by the traitorous habit of the Irish informers—such as we have in every liberation movement—against the committed nationalists; but the anger which takes him away from the cause also makes him even more complicit in the fate of the land and people because he has the advantage of knowledge which the pioneers did not have. Referring to Ireland as "the old sow that eats her farrow" (Joyce, 1969, p. 188), Stephen ignores the fact that this despicable Irish image is also the product of colonial force against which the natives were helpless. As in every case of colonial conquest, resistance strategies refine themselves over time, are never consensual, and are often derailed by factional interests. A purist whose pride is so exclusive it cannot admit the possibility of failure, Stephen is simply fulfilling the agenda of the colonialist by destroying the basis of a common platform.

CONCLUSION

A Portrait ends with reference to two significant places, Dublin and Trieste, which recall the desire of modernism's Bohemians to travel all over continental Europe. While their dating, 1904 and 1914 respectively, marks the time span within which the novel was written, giving it a relatively epic dimension, it is the dairy entries of the last two days that reveal the way Stephen has transformed physical space into a psychological variant, and in this way reinvents an imaginary Ireland for his creative purpose. The strength of *A Portrait* as a modernist text lies in this reinvention of space in which Ireland is imagined and textualized mainly in the mind of the protagonist and thus becomes a "picture of [his] spiritual self" (Bulson, 2006, p. 17). Urging himself to get "Away! Away!" into the unrestrictive but deprived space of exile, Stephen characteristically reflects on the ambiguous "spell of arms and voices" which (if taken as Irish folks) endeavour to hold him back in the hope that he would acknowledge the validity of Irish folklore which he has repeatedly faulted without providing a valid or convincing alternative; and simultaneously seduce him (now as the Sirens of exile) away from the constraining surroundings into imagined freedom. Davin had already diagnosed his flaw: "In heart you are an Irishman but your pride is too powerful" (Joyce, 1969, p. 188). Like the mythical Icarus that he seems to emulate, the culturally unconscionable flight into exile may only end with his imaginative wings melting in humiliation. This doomed possibility is because "the spell of arms and voices" is acknowledged as the exilic momentum to his recalcitrant spirit, already imagining "their promise of close embraces and ... their tale of distant nations" (Joyce, 1969, p. 234). These latter are his new "kinsmen," real only in a symbolic sense, and represent the delusionary base for his new vision. Ironically, then, "Stephen can achieve his independence only by imagining that the entire city of Dublin is out to betray him" (Bulson, 2006, p. 52). In other words, he willingly allows his imagination to run away with him literally, and his fears are framed eloquently against the national community.

In this regard, Valente (1995, p. 37) censures critical obsession over "Stephen's rejection of Ireland and the Irish cause" and concludes that "it would perhaps be truer to speak of a mutual polarisation, in which the nationalist refusal to tolerate analysis or ambivalence, let alone opposition, helps to push Stephen toward a stance of elitist apostasy." I find this too much of a concession to Stephen's proud disposition, placing him at par with the community of nationalists who choose to stay and endure the brunt of colonial violence. Stephen's empathy with "distant nations" is as flattering to his ego as it is escapist, if not deceitful, between which he romanticises the hope of exile without investigating into the possibly intricate histories of such nations beyond the packaged history of, say, the Romans. His mother—whose voice is the last to be slighted by Stephen—is not just the biological representative of all that

Stephen is abandoning, she is also Mother Ireland, in revivalist terms, and he, the proud, ungrateful son.

If in Trieste Joyce "became interested in the question of confessional writing and its reception" (Nash, 2006, p. 70), it is possibly because its collocation with Stephen's "distant nations" problematises the protagonist's sacrifice of physical environment for an illusionary version, which is brought to live only in his imagination. The invoked "Old artificer" rhymes in opposition with his rejection of motherly plea and suggests Stephen's need for a symbolic father who can authenticate his new status more than his biological father. His anticipation of a new life is therefore misleading because the anticipated "encounter for the millionth time [with] the reality of experience" is envisaged in denial of organic data and not rooted in the experience of his people and culture. As such, "the smithy of my soul" in which he hopes to forge "the uncreated conscience of my race" (Joyce, 1969, p. 235) becomes the site of his objectified arrogance, claiming redemptive potentials for the abandoned race.

The postcolonial implications of reading the politics of spatial nationalism in *A Portrait* thus reveal the imperative of identity as inseparable from even a modernist imagination. As I have suggested, Yeats' complementary aesthetics evolved in this militant direction by indulging stylistic innovation only as a means of refin(d)ing his roots. In Joyce's novel, on the other hand, space and identity are exploited as collateral to the assertion of an imagined abstractness which conflates Anglo-Irish historicity into a mental elixir. Unlike nationalist concerns with finite space within which issues are highlighted and resolved, albeit often idealistically, Stephen instead contemplates change by abandoning the very setting for such a possibility. By relating to space in this way, Stephen compromises the very hope for Irish identity that his narrative highlights as a cultural need.

REFERENCES

Attridge, D. (2000). *Joyce Effects. On Language, Theory, and History*. Cambridge University Press.

Bulson, E. (2006). *The Cambridge Introduction to James Joyce*. Cambridge University Press.

Dettmar, K. J. H. (2004). Introduction, *A Portrait of The Artist as a Young Man and Dubliners*. Sterling Publishing. (xiii-xxx)

Ellmann, M. (2010). *The Nets of Modernism: Henry James, Virginia Woolf, James Joyce, and Sigmund Freud*. Cambridge University Press.

Fisk, L. A. (2004). *Exploration of the Outer Heliosphere and the Local Interstellar*

Medium: A Workshop Report. National Research Council.

Frye, N. (2000). *Anatomy of Criticism Four Essays.* Princeton University Press.

Jackson, A. (2004). Ireland, the Union, and the Empire, 1800-1960. In K. Kevin (Ed.), *Ireland and the British Empire.* (pp. 123-153). Oxford University Press.

Jameson, F. (1981). *The Political Unconscious: Narrative as a Socially Symbolic Act.* Cornell University Press.

Joyce, J. (1969). *A Portrait of the Artist as a Young Man.* Heinemann.

Joyce, J. (2000). *Ulysses.* Penguin.

Kilberd, D. (1996). *Inventing Ireland: The Literature of a Modern Nation.* Vintage.

Kilberd, D. (2005). *The Irish Writer and the World.* Cambridge University Press.

Large, W. (2015). *Levinas: Totality and Infinity.* Bloomsbury Academic.

Levinas, E. (1999). *Alterity and Transcendence.* Athlone Press.

Levinas, E. (1989). *The Levinas Reader.* Ed Sean Hand. Blackwell.

Marcus, P. (2008). *Being for the Other: Emmanuel Levinas, Ethical Living and Psychoanalysis.* Marquette University Press.

Nash, J. (2006). *James Joyce and the Act of Reception: Reading, Ireland, Modernism.* Cambridge University Press.

Nolan, E. (1995). *James Joyce and Nationalism.* Routledge.

O'Rourke, B. (2011). *Galician and Irish in the European Context: Attitudes towards Weak and Strong Minority Languages.* Palgrave-Macmillan.

Pellin, N. (2003). *Anglo-Irish Relations, 1798-1922.* Routledge.

Valente, J. (1995). *James Joyce and the Problem of Justice: Negotiating Sexual and Colonial Difference.* Cambridge University Press.

Woolf, V. (1999). *To the Lighthouse.* Oxford University Press.

4

Male Assertion and the Arts in Virginia Woolf's *To the Lighthouse*

ERNEST L. VEYU

One of Virginia Woolf's concerns in *To the Lighthouse* is on art, and she gives quite a central narrative space to it. Artists have unveiled much of the story's events, and their art is symbolic in many ways. The novel itself is a work of art produced by an artist – Virginia Woolf. Ruby Cohn beautifully puts this fact through with the assertion that *To the Lighthouse* "is a work of art about art" (Lewis 1994, p. 63).

Since the essay is dedicated to examining how the arts are affected by male assertiveness in *To the Lighthouse*, we shall begin by looking at the expression "Male Assertion." Pfafman (2017), in her article titled "Assertiveness," purports that: "Assertiveness involves expressing ideas, feelings, and boundaries while respecting others' rights, maintaining a positive effect on the receiver, and considering potential consequences of the expression." Assertion goes along with synonyms such as, "affirmation, asseveration, avouchment, avowal, claim, declaration, insistence, profession, and protestation." Male assertiveness, therefore, consists of the man behaving confidently, authoritatively, and assuming several rights over the woman, mainly on the basis of his being male. It consists of recognition, honour, and respect because one is male, not female.

On the other hand, *The Encyclopaedia Britannica* defines art as: "The use of skill and imagination in the creation of aesthetic objects, environments, or experiences that can be shared with others." According to this definition, art demands skill and imagination for creative purposes. Also, that which has been created may be objects, environments, or experiences capable of being shared. The *Oxford Languages and Google* define art as "the expression or application of human creative skill and imagination, typically in a visual form such as painting or sculpture, producing works to be appreciated primarily for their beauty or emotional power." Art expresses human creative skills and imagination, irrespective of gender. It is the product of human natural endowment, expressed aesthetically. In *To the Lighthouse*, we can think of Lily Briscoe's painting, Carmichael's poetry, and Mrs Ramsay's art of life. In the following lines, we shall look at men and the arts, women and the arts, and then at Virginia Woolf's portrait of men and women.

MEN AND THE ARTS

In a phallocracy, as is the case in *To the Lighthouse*, that which carries honour, dignity, and respect, belongs to the male. Such domains are either made strictly taboo for women, or women are simply made to believe that it is unwomanly to partake of them. On the contrary, man is allowed the monopoly of acquiring the great cultural values and personal cultivation derived from involvement in such domains. In *To the Lighthouse*, art is one such domain, especially because of its positive effects on the artist.

Art fulfils the artist to the point where he or she has no time for other pleasures in life. Lily Briscoe "would always go on painting, because it interested her" (60). She has no room for riches, love, marriage, and materialism. Art provides one with a sense of wholesomeness and makes them feel useful. Through his/her work, the artist is assured that he/she has contributed something that can be shared with others. This allows for the building of self-esteem that enhances psychic balance. In Freudian thinking, art helps the artist to release repressed desires, whose energy would be disruptive to the harmonious functioning of the personality.

Furthermore, there is a quality to art in which the practitioner cultivates himself, thus enriching his thought and experience. For example, Mrs Ramsay, as an artist of life, seems to understand the nature of life more than anyone else in *To the Lighthouse*. When we first meet Mr Carmichael, "he is an odious solitary melancholic man." But at the end of the novel, with the writing and publication of his volume of poetry, Lily Briscoe testifies that "She knew him in that way. She knew that he had changed somehow" (164). Involvement with art and succeeding in creating objects, environments, or experiences that can be shared positively transforms the artist psychologically, especially.

In *To the Lighthouse*, the importance of art and its superiority to the other disciplines is evident. By virtue of this superiority of place, man has made the domain of art, the sphere of male jurisdiction. Charles Tansley's "Women can't paint, women can't write" is a determined male attempt to exclude women from the arts of writing and painting. Becoming a male-dominated sphere, art lacks the feminine touch that should help to give it full bloom. This is evident in Mr Carmichael's poetry: "It was about the desert and the camel. It was about the palm tree and the sunset. It said something about death; it said very little about love" (164). The images in Carmichael's poetry transmit a message of sterility and barrenness; the "desert" lacks fertility, vegetation and water. The "camel" is a desert animal that has been plagued by harsh desert conditions for so long that it has become adapted to them. This is probably reflective of Mr Carmichael's experience in the world because he has gone from one unfortunate situation to another before settling to write poetry. He is already acquainted with life's hardships, as the camel is with the conditions of the desert.

Still, in relation to the images in Carmichael's poetry, the "palm tree" represents solitude, and the "sunset" talks of desperateness, old age, and belatedness. The impersonality of the poetry transmits a message of lost personal values and a loss of self-awareness. The "little about love" reminds one of the good old days, which are deteriorating into an end in "death." Once more, these images are reflective of Mr Carmichael. He is old, lonely, and frustrated by his experience of life and looks forward to the grave. His poetry lacks a feminine touch so that it stands out as half-finished. A female touch would have brought in an element of life, more love, a greater sense of self, and an oasis in the desert of his life. This, however, is lacking because he has rejected women and all that is womanly in an attempt to assert himself.

Looking at the example of Carmichael, poetry in the hands of a chauvinist is unwholesome, leaving a sense of being half-baked. It gives a partial view of the possibilities of poetry because it is presented from one point of view, the male's, expressing only the deleterious aspects of life. It goes without saying that male-dominated art will only present the world and life as man perceives them. On the whole, the values upheld will be male-oriented, and its themes will revolve around chivalry, hardship, bravery, conquest, and adventure.

WOMEN AND THE ARTS

In *To the Lighthouse*, a man represents a barrier to any outstanding artistic endeavour for a woman. Virginia Woolf, while mourning her father's departure from this world, is nevertheless happy because his remaining alive would have meant for her – "no writing, no books." This suggests that the father was somewhat of an obstacle to her writing career. In *To the Lighthouse*, Lily Briscoe has to leave her father's house before indulging in painting. If she remains at home, she will not be allowed to paint because she has to be "keeping house for her father off the Brompton Road" (17). Actually, her refusal to marry is partly because she cannot successfully be "always taking care of some man" (6) and yet produce good paintings. When she has to "keep house and sit beside sleeping children indoors" (138), she cannot at the same time accomplish her artistic vision. Love and marriage, in themselves, are not bad, but a husband's demands and the responsibility of raising many children rule out the woman from the arts.

In Chopin's (2008) *The Awakening,* Mademoiselle Reiz, a female artist in a patriarchal milieu, once said: *"To be an artist includes much. One must possess many gifts- absolute gifts- which have not been acquired by one's own effort. And, moreover, to succeed, the artist must possess the courageous soul… The brave soul. The soul that dares and defies"* (p. 68). True to the above, the female artistic soul of Lily Briscoe, for instance, has to "dare" to do that which is believed to be for men only. It also has to defy laid-down traditional notions that artistic involvement and productivity are not for women. In this way, the female artist is flooded with a sense of conflict and guilt in the exercise of that which she possesses by natural endowments.

When the female artist has to fight against male-asserting conventions, she dispenses a lot of physical and psychic energy, so that before she actually settles down to work, her potential has already been greatly curtailed. Her work, both qualitatively and quantitatively, is brought below the cream. Lily Briscoe's difficulties in this area are expressed as follows, "And it was then too, in that chill and windy way, as she began to paint, there forced themselves upon her other things, her own inadequacy, her insignificance, keeping house for her father and much ado to control her impulse" (23). In this passage, Lily Briscoe suffers most from the constant reminders by the men of her shortcomings and the low esteem of women in her society. The discouraging comments made by the men haunt her just at the moment when she begins to paint, so her painting becomes mediocre, at least in her mind, in many ways.

Lily Briscoe's painting in the first part of the novel is aimed at producing a picture of Mrs Ramsay and James. As she works on her painting, there comes a moment when she decides to "move the tree rather more to the middle"(84). Earlier on, Mrs Ramsay has been leaning on this tree that she is reproducing, so moving the tree from the periphery to the middle is an artistic endeavour to give the woman a central place. Her art is consequently made to serve a feminist cause. It is bound to be partial, biased, and to represent life as desired rather than as it really is. Art, rather than being an exercise of the creative powers of the individual, becomes a warfare tool between the sexes. There is a sense in which Briscoe's commitment to painting and to completing her painting is a challenge to the male-asserting notion that women can neither paint nor write. When she finishes her painting, she has proven the worth of her sex.

It is said of Lily Briscoe that "the war had drawn the sting of her femininity" (134). Her consciousness and awareness of herself as a woman have been reawakened, and finding that she too shares the plight of every woman, she lets her sting out for war. Since her feminine sting has been drawn, she has a sense of hostility towards the men in her life. Her painting in the last part of the novel is a determined effort to make life standstill so that she may understand and subdue it.

Lily Briscoe and Carmichael are both artists living in the same house. One would expect these two to take advantage of living together to share and exchange artistic views. But they do not. The awkwardness of this situation disturbs Lily Briscoe, so she keeps asking, "Why always be drawn out and haled away? Why not left in peace, to talk to Mr Carmichael on the lawn?" (133). Her inability to relate to and talk to Mr Carmichael implies that her art falls short of the element that should have come from him. Rather than work together as artists, she says the situation "roused one to perpetual combat, challenged one to a fight in which one was bound to be worsted" (133). Furthermore;

> Always (it was in her nature, or in her sex, she did not know which) before she exchanged the fluidity of life for the concentration of painting she had a few moments of nakedness when she seemed like an unborn soul, a soul reft of body, hesitating on some windy pinnacle and exposed without protection to all the blasts of doubt. Why then did she do it? She looked at the canvas, lightly scored with running lines. It would be hung in the servants' bedrooms. It would be rolled up and stuffed under a sofa. What was the good of doing it then, and she heard some voice saying she couldn't paint, saying she couldn't create, as if she were caught up in one of those habitual currents in which after a certain time experience forms in the mind, so that one repeats words without being aware any longer who originally spoke them. In this perpetual combat, not only is she and her sex "worsted," but also her art, because art depends on the artist (133).

The war between the sexes, especially in the domain of art, meant that Lily Briscoe, along with all the other women are in a combat that leaves them exposed and weakened. In her painting, she is "exposed without protection to all the blasts of doubt." Furthermore, she meditates on the fate of the finished product of female painting – "It would be hung in the servants' bedrooms. It would be rolled up and stuffed under a sofa." This means that if patriarchy failed to stop the woman from painting, it would vilify the finished product. This is reason enough to discourage any female artist. She concludes that "In this perpetual combat, not only is she and her sex 'worsted', but also her art, because art depends on the artist" (133).

While Lily Briscoe is under the weight of the above, her counterpart male artist, Mr Carmichael, is on a clean path to fame and honour for publishing a volume of poetry. Lily Briscoe "remembered, smiling at the slipper that dangled from his foot. People said that his poetry was 'so beautiful.' They went and published things he had written forty years ago. There was a famous man now called Carmichael" (164). He is widely read and acclaimed, but no one ever knows about Lily Briscoe and her painting in any significant way. Consequently, the societal spectrum for art becomes partial, incomplete, and wanting since artistic productions by women are variously flawed and barred from the general public.

In the novel's early pages, mention is made of some male artists who had visited a particular site and made a scene for admiration. Mrs Ramsay tells the story of one of them, "in Panama hat and yellow boots, seriously, and softly, absorbedly… with an air of profound contentment on his round red face, gazing, and then, when he had gazed, dipping imbuing, the tip of his brush in some soft mound of green or pink" (11). The details given bespeak the spectacle that their visit must have produced. In this case of biased attention, both the male artist and his art are objects of general admiration. The male artist receives all the acclamation, and his morale is raised for better artistic productions, while the female artist, Lily Briscoe, has to stop painting or turn away her painting from intruding men. Guigou (2015, p. 3) affirms that in *To the Lighthouse*, the "creative female identity fights to adapt to male-dominated spaces." We can safely say that in a phallocracy, as in *To the Lighthouse*, female art thrives only in solitude and in the hidden.

Another point to note is the fact that the pattern of Lily Briscoe's art in *To the Lighthouse* is essentially masculine; "Since Mr Paunceforth had been there, three years before, all the pictures were like that, she said, green and grey, with lemon-coloured sailing-boats, and pink women on the beach" (11). When Lily Briscoe begins her painting of Mrs Ramsay, she follows the Paunceforth style. It is only afterwards that she emancipates into abstract art, under severe criticism from Mr Bankes. Apart from giving a pattern to both male and female art, the portrait of the women in the Paunceforth pattern is unbecoming; "pink women on the beach." The image of the woman in the dominant art of the day ties in with Mr Ramsay's opinion of women: "They never got anything worth having from one year's end to another. They did nothing but talk, talk, talk, eat, eat, eat. It was the women's fault. Women made civilisation impossible with all their "charm," all their silliness" (72). This is seen in the fact that the women in the Paunceforth art pattern have become pink for spending all their time or most of it idly lying on the beach in the sun's rays.

Notably, none of the Ramsay girls take up an artistic career; in fact, no other woman does. The future for female art is therefore quite bleak. By extrapolation, it is probable that the day Lily Briscoe dies, female art dies with her. The lesser arts, those less notable for inspiring only a little honour, fame, and importance, are left to women and children. Mrs Ramsay may exercise her reading skills to James as she wishes. She may cut out pictures from printed pages with James or let him do it alone; no one cares. She may finish the knitting of her stocking or not; it's no other person's business. But let her leave the major arts to the men.

Male assertion has so far been shown to have a marked negative influence on female art. It has also been shown that the full spectrum and possibility of art has been lowered because a significant female part has been labelled "inferior" and kept aside for the most part. Furthermore, there is an apparent effort to discourage women from engaging in any significant amount of artistic practice. In many ways, this has flawed art as a whole, whether produced by men or women.

VIRGINIA WOOLF'S PORTRAIT OF MEN AND WOMEN

In the novel *To the Lighthouse*, it is said of women that they can neither write nor paint. However, Lily Briscoe does paint in defiance of that declaration. There is a sense in which no woman needs to write in the novel because the novel itself is written by a woman. This alone is enough to prove the fact that women can both read and write. She is basically feminist in her whole approach to *To the Lighthouse*. She is often listed, along with Simone de Beauvoir, as belonging to the first wave of the feminist movement (Campbell, 2000, p. 23). In *To the Lighthouse*, therefore, she lets out in reaction to patriarchy and every form of injustice done to women. In this section of the article, we are interested in her portraits of men and women. The men she creates and the character traits she gives them tell of what she thinks of them. We shall begin by looking at her portrait of men.

The opening pages of *To the Lighthouse* give a pretty bizarre picture of Mr Ramsay. From the description of his appearance, one is already suspicious of some evil in him: "lean as a knife, narrow as the blade of one, grinning sarcastically, not only with the pleasure of disillusioning his son and casting ridicule upon his wife, who was ten thousand times better in every way than he was (James thought), but also with some secret conceit at his own accuracy of judgement" (4-5). The images of "a knife" and "the blade of one" are immediately suggestive of harm, torture, and wounding. This is soon followed by the detail that he grins sarcastically and takes pleasure in disillusioning his son and ridiculing his wife, whereas his wife was many times better than him. He is further described as follows: "He is petty, selfish, vain, egotistical; he is spoilt; he is a tyrant; he wears Mrs Ramsay to death" (21). He has an "astonishing lack of consideration for other people's feelings" (28). He is at the root of his wife's early death. Mrs Ramsay: "She has the wisdom of Forster's Mrs Wilcox and Mrs Moore, who know and are, but instead of living to eighty-six or ninety as such women do, Mrs Ramsay also dies young in her late fifties" (159). Lily Briscoe, referring to Mr Ramsay, says: "That man, she thought, her anger rising in her, never gave; that man took. She [Mrs Ramsay], on the other hand, would be forced to give. Mrs Ramsay had given. Giving, giving, giving, she had died—and had left all this" (126). Virginia Woolf's Mr Ramsay is a bad man, petty, selfish, vain, egotistical, spoilt, a tyrant, inconsiderate, selfish, exploitative, sadist and the like. He is irritable, touchy, and happy after saying the most melancholic things. He is abusive to his wife and makes stringent demands on those around him.

Virginia Woolf also paints a near-rapist picture of Mr Ramsay. As Lily Briscoe says, "this was one of those moments when an enormous need urged him, without being conscious of what it was, to approach any woman, to force them, he did not care how, his need was so great, to give him what he wanted: sympathy" (127). The idea of approaching any woman and possibly forcing her, suppose that female consent is not an option for Mr Ramsay. When his wife dies, his sudden change of attitude towards Lily Briscoe and Cam (his daughter) is very much linked to his sexual hankerings. The following lines express some sexual pressure he puts on Lily Briscoe just before taking the expedition to the lighthouse:

> He sighed significantly. All Lily wished was that this enormous flood of grief, this insatiable hunger for sympathy, this demand that she should surrender herself up to him entirely, and even though he had sorrows enough to keep her supplied for ever, should leave her, should be diverted (she kept looking at the house, hoping for an interruption) before it swept her down in its flow (127-128).

The passage above portrays Mr Ramsay in desperate need of sympathy, a euphemism for sexual desire, which Virginia Woolf very often uses about Mr Ramsay's lascivious longings. The fact that in this episode, she keeps looking at the house, hoping for an interruption, betrays her fears that Mr Ramsay could possibly force her into a sexual relationship. Virginia Woolf further describes the scene as follows:

> They stood there, isolated from the rest of the world. His immense self-pity, his demand for sympathy poured and spread itself in pools at her feet, and all she did, miserable sinner that she was, was to draw her skirts a little closer round her ankles, lest she should get wet. In complete silence she stood there, grasping her paint brush (128).

The passage above suggests that Mr Ramsay actually gets Lily Briscoe into a sexual mood, in which case she is afraid she could get sexually wet. Virginia Woolf says Mr Ramsay's demand for sympathy poured and spread itself in pools at Lily Briscoe's feet. It is a case of sexual harassment, where Mr Ramsay takes advantage of the fact that the place where Briscoe is painting is isolated, and they are only the two of them.

Unlike what he had expected, Mr Ramsay's books do not make him popular. Therefore, he carries a sense of failure and despair. His philosophical talks to the young men of Cardiff (about Locke, Hume, Berkeley, and the causes of the French Revolution) are termed "some nonsense." In his philosophic pursuits, he becomes so odious that his wife prefers boobies more, because they did not bother one with their dissertations. Furthermore:

> all had to be deprecated and concealed under the phrase "talking nonsense," because, in effect, he had not done the thing he might have done. It was a disguise; it was the refuge of a man afraid to own his own feelings, who could not say, This is what I like—this is what I am; and rather pitiable and distasteful to William Bankes and Lily Briscoe, who wondered why such concealments should be necessary; why he needed always praise; why so brave a man in thought should be so timid in life; how strangely he was venerable and laughable at one and the same time (38).

The lines above sum up Mr Ramsay as a failure in his own eyes, and in the eyes of those around him. Even though he has some academic accomplishments to his advantage, they fall very far short of his lofty expectations in life. He is venerable in terms of being a university professor but also laughable in relation to the mastery of life outside the classroom.

In another male portrait, Mr Charles Tansley is shown as offensive by his very person: "He was such a miserable specimen, the children said, all humps and hollows ... he was a sarcastic brute" (7). Also, "when they talked about something, people, music, history, anything ... until he had turned the whole thing round and made it somehow reflect himself and disparage them, put them all on edge somehow with his acid way of peeling the flesh and blood off everything, he was not satisfied" (7). This reveals that both Mr Tansley is essentially narrow-minded and egotistical. He is described as a miserable specimen, a sarcastic brute, and something of an ill-fed person. He is, in every way, unpleasant. In the matter of the journey to the lighthouse, his language is aggressive against Mrs Ramsay and James Ramsay: "He was a sarcastic brute, Andrew said" (7). Mr Bankes describes him as follows: "He seemed to be rather cocksure, this young man; and his manners were bad" (78).

As mentioned above, Charles Tansley is sarcastic and underrates other people. For all the help Mrs Ramsay has given him, he imagines her recompense to be a cab fare, had they been in one. This kind of thinking can only come from "that poor young man" (27), whom he is. All he has to count upon is "the influence of somebody upon something" (55) and his "ugly academic jargon" (7) of dissertation, fellowship, readership and lectureship. Talking about him, Mrs Ramsay prays: "Pray Heaven he won't fall in love with Prue," (55) and her husband adds: "He'd disinherit her if she married him, said Mr Ramsay" (55). In the later part of the novel, Lily Briscoe meets him preaching brotherly love by "denouncing something: he was condemning somebody" (166). His notion of brotherly love is that which denounces and condemns somebody. This is ridiculing: "Everything about him had that meagre fixity, that bare unloveliness," (77) and yet he had the guts to preach brotherly love. Overall, Charles Tansley is disgusting, unpleasant and socially unfit.

Augustus Carmichael, another of Woolf's male characters in *To the Lighthouse*, is the embodiment of clumsiness: "He was unkempt; he dropped things on his coat; he had the tiresomeness of an old man with nothing in the world to do" (35). He has taken opium till staining his beard yellow: "He said nothing. He took opium. The children said he had stained his beard yellow with it" (35). Hardly does he say anything to anybody. At supper, he is the only one who asks for a second plate of soup and is very oblivious of what people think of him. His gluttonous tendency annoys Mr Ramsay but he does not notice it at all. He detests Mrs Ramsay, yet depends on her for food and shelter. After his meal, "he would lie all day long on the lawn brooding presumably over his poetry till he reminded one of a cat watching birds (80). He is a victim of an early and unfortunate marriage that crushed all his ambitions. Mrs Ramsay tells the story of "an affair at Oxford with some girl; an early marriage; poverty; ... but what really was the use of that?—and then lying, as they saw him, on the lawn" (9). With the failure of the affair and the marriage, his life lacks direction; from the great philosopher he would have been, he travels to India, translates some poetry, and teaches Persian and Hindustani. But, on the whole, he is a failure. Although he publishes a volume of poetry, his life amounts to very little, as he remains dependent on the charity of the Ramsays.

The most moderate picture of a man in *To the Lighthouse* is that of William Bankes. Yet his uprightness becomes his undoing. It makes him proud, putting on the airs of Jane Austen's Mr Darcy in *Pride and Prejudice*. He hates family life and does not make friends. He is comparatively richer than Mr Ramsay but lives alone. Mrs Ramsay thinks the following about him:

> William Bankes—poor man! who had no wife, and no children and dined alone in lodgings except for tonight; and in pity for him, life being now strong enough to bear her on again, she began all this business, as a sailor not without weariness sees the wind fill his sail and yet hardly wants to be off again and thinks how, had the ship sunk, he would have whirled round and round and found rest on the floor of the sea (70-71).

Mrs Ramsay describes him as poor, without a wife or children, solitary, lonely, and demotivated, almost suicidal. In his own words, "private life was disagreeable" (78). After losing his wife, life has never been the same for him, and he vows never to get married again. He finds family life, like the case of Mr Ramsay, very disgusting. He is critical of government, Lily Briscoe's art, and virtually everything else.

Summarily, there is nothing to admire about the men of *To the Lighthouse*. They fail in life and lack the basic aspects of social and civic life. Their actions are a psychological cover-up to make the women folk respect them. This said, we shall consider the portrait of women by Virginia Woolf. All the women in *To the Lighthouse* are victims of the male assertive tradition in which they find themselves. They are generally good women with a clear sense of commitment and direction. Irrespective of their suffering, they do whatever they have to do well. What follows is an attempt to examine Virginia Woolf's presentation of them.

Virginia Woolf presents Mrs Ramsay through the image of the "straddling wings." She is portrayed as "a hen straddling her wings out in protection of a covey of little chicks"(18). This talks of her commitment to keeping and protecting her eight children. Her success in this task is enormous because, until after her death, no harm or evil befalls any of her children. Her protecting wings are also extended to cover the men:

> She had the whole of the other sex under her protection; for reasons she could not explain, for their chivalry and valour, for the fact that they negotiated treaties, ruled India, controlled finance; finally for an attitude towards herself which no woman could fail to feel or to find agreeable, something trustful, childlike, reverential; which an old woman could take from a young man without loss of dignity, and woe betide the girl—pray Heaven it was none of her daughters!—who did not feel the worth of it, and all that it implied, to the marrow of her bones (6)!

Unlike the intrinsically exploitative husband, Mrs Ramsay cares for all the men. She valorises them because they negotiated treaties, ruled India, and controlled finance. She is trustful, honest and reverential in her whole attitude. Although the men are hardly cooperative, she does her work dutifully, with unwavering commitment. In another image, she is presented as having a "delicious fecundity" and a "fountain and spray of life": "As if all her energies were being fused into force, burning and illuminating… and into this delicious fecundity, this fountain and spray of life, the fatal sterility of the male plunged itself, like a beak of brass, barren and bare" (38). She is presented as the response, par excellence, to male sterility. She is the fertilising alternative of the barrenness induced by the men. She represents the source and nurture of life. It is her fecundity that fertilises the fatally sterile male. She is full of energy and vigour and imparts life to the men.

Her greatest strength is her submission to her husband. This is because she wins her husband's favour at the end, giving him no reason for any genuine complaint against her. By submission, she wins, as her desire for the journey to the lighthouse is fulfilled. From her position of submission, she "resolved everything into simplicity; made angers, irritations fall off like old rags; she brought together this and that and then this, and so made out of that miserable silliness and spite…something" (135). She brings simplicity to modern life's complicatedness, resolves angers and irritations, and holds her family and the long list of visitors in unity.

In *To the Lighthouse*, Virginia Woolf not only paints Mrs Ramsay as an all-capable woman, but she also makes her into a light. When she looked at the light of the lighthouse, it "had her at its beck and call":

> She saw the light again. With some irony in her interrogation, for when

> one woke at all, one's relations changed, she looked at the steady light, the pitiless, the remorseless, which was so much her, yet so little her, which had her at its beck and call ... watching it with fascination, hypnotised, as if it were stroking with its silver fingers some sealed vessel in her brain whose bursting would flood her with delight, she had known happiness, exquisite happiness, intense happiness, and it silvered the rough waves a little more brightly, as daylight faded, and the blue went out of the sea and it rolled in waves of pure lemon which curved and swelled and broke upon the beach and the ecstasy burst in her eyes and waves of pure delight raced over the floor of her mind and she felt, It is enough! It is enough (15)!

The symbolic three rays of light from the top of the lighthouse represent Mrs Ramsay. When she looks at the rays, Woolf notes: "the steady light, the pitiless, the remorseless, which was so much her, yet so little her, which had her at its beck and call." She is herself, light, and the light is at her beck and call. She is light, commands light and the light beckons to her. She so identifies with the light that "she looked up over her knitting and met the third stroke and it seemed to her like her own eyes meeting her own eyes" (53). Then, "She praised herself in praising the light, without vanity, for she was stern, she was searching, she was beautiful like that light" (53). She is the light to her husband, children and all else. She gives direction and orients men as the lighthouse's light does.

Another female character, Lily Briscoe, is full of determination and a sense of purpose. She is a very decisive person. When she decides not to marry, she sticks to her decision despite Mrs Ramsay's encouragement. She has her convictions about what love ought to be and does not bow to Mr Bankes' approaches. She prefers the "love that never attempted to clutch its object; but, like the love that mathematicians bear their symbols, or poets their phrases, was meant to be spread over the world and become part of the human gain" (40). She prefers the love that leaves her time to paint and to be in control of her life. The novel ends with, "I have had my vision," which is also the triumphant note with which Lily Briscoe ends her painting. It is also what remains in the reader's mind as he finishes reading the novel. She is a success.

Minta Doyle, another female character, is also presented very positively in *To the Lighthouse*. She is a very outgoing person, beautiful and attractive. She comes to the Ramsay home at Mrs Ramsay's invitation and associates efficiently with every family member and visitor. Throughout the story, she gets affianced to and marries Paul Rayley. She makes a mess of her marriage, leading her husband to seek satisfaction in a mistress. But this relationship with the mistress, "far from breaking up the marriage…had righted it. They were excellent friends, obviously, as he sat on the road and she handed him his tools" (146). She is not the worst for her unbecoming conduct. Her errors are easily pardonable, and she does not hurt everyone else as do the men.

CONCLUSION

Virginia Woolf's portrait of the men shows them as chauvinistic, insensitive, assertive, clumsy, ugly, violent, sterile, venerable, and syllogistic. On the other hand, the women are generous, caring, loving, tender, self-sacrificing, and other such beautiful descriptions. This, for sure, is a partial rendition by an artist who has taken sides in a war of the sexes. It turns her novel into feminist propaganda. Such art and artists have undergone a twist, falling short of the glory of genuine art and artists.

Farooq (2020, p. 7) suggests that "Woolf's iconic vision does not subscribe to the partisan approach." In her feminism, "she seeks to bring sanity to the unjust distribution of prestige and privilege among the sexes… she also undoes the rigidity of heterosexual orthodoxy (7). Furthermore, "Woolf breaks the rigid system of gender categorisation by working on the determinants of gender and showing that these determinants are largely performative and do not refer back to any innate essence or genealogical etymology" (3).

For art to attain its full expression, the artist must be able to attain androgyny, "a specific way of joining the 'masculine' and 'feminine' aspects of a single human being" (Singer 1977, p. 22). From a macroscopic point of view, a society attains androgyny when its men and women can come together harmoniously. Failure to achieve this state of affairs is primarily due to the male's desire to assert himself over the woman. Singer further says, "Androgyny, however, corresponds more faithfully to the guiding human archetype, than does a societal structure based on a dominantly patriarchal mode of functioning with woman in a subordinate role" (22). Elizabeth Wright holds that "Androgyny, for Virginia Woolf, was a theory that aimed to offer men and women the chance to write without consciousness of their sex – the result of which would ideally result in uninhibited creativity" (1).

In *To the Lighthouse*, the disharmony between the sexes created by the male's desire to assert himself negatively affects art. At the beginning of the novel, Lily Briscoe is very conscious of the subservient existence of Mrs Ramsay to Mr Ramsay. She complains about it and withdraws from all involvement with men. She is literally at war with the other sex. She is unable to achieve androgyny as an individual because, by rejecting the man, she has rejected the "masculine" aspect of her personality. Consequently, she lacks androgynous wholesomeness, and this is reflected in the relatively unsuccessful painting that she produces. In the novel's third part, she begins to change her position against the men as Mr Ramsay weakens in his tyrannical treatment of women. She accepts Mr Ramsay and actually follows him in her mind on their journey to the lighthouse. In accepting Mr Ramsay, she also accepts the "masculine" part of herself. She, therefore, attains the androgynous state that permits her to accomplish her vision. Fau (2019, p. 8) holds that, "Thanks to Lily's artful vision, they had their voyage out, to and past the lighthouse."

REFERENCES

Austen, J. (2018). *Pride and Prejudice*. Global Grey, globalgreyebooks.com, https://www. pdfdrive.com/pride-and-prejudice-d49696146.html.

Campbell, J. (2000). *Arguing with the Phallus Feminist, Queer and Postcolonial Theory: A Psychoanalytic Contribution*, London: Zed Books.

Chopin, K. (2008). *The Awakening and Selected Short Stories*, A Penn State Electronic Classics Series Publication, https://www.pdfdrive.com/the-awakening-kate-chopin-d31468401.html.

Njamsi, M. E. (1990). The Recurrent Images in Women's Fiction: A Study of Kate Chopin's *The Awakening*, Virginia Woolf's *To the Lighthouse* and Alice Walker's *The Color Purple*, M. A. Dissertation, Yaounde University.

Fau, H. (2019). The 'One-Line-Portrait' in *To The Lighthouse* By Virginia Woolf: Freeing the Counter-Norms, pp. 1-8. Sciendo DOI: 10.2478/genst-2019-0001, https://sciendo.com/ pdf/10.2478/genst--0001

Graubard, A. (2019). The Tyrant Father: Leslie Stephen and Masculine Influences on Virginia Woolf and her Novel, *To the Lighthouse*" Honors Theses, University of Nebraska-Lincoln. 96. http://digitalcommons.unl.edu/honorstheses/96.

Guigou, I. M. (2015). Women Creators: Artistry and Sacrifice in the Novels of Virginia Woolf. *FIU Electronic Theses and Dissertations. 2250*. https://digitalcommons.fiu.edu/etd/2250.

Lewis, S. W. (1975). *Virginia Woolf: A Collection of Criticism*, New York: McGraw-Hill.

Muluh, G. (1994). The Woman as a Proficient Artist of Life, Dissertation, University of Yaounde 1, Dissertation, ENS Yaounde, June.

Pfafman T. (2017). Assertiveness. *Springer International*. Pp. 1-8.

Farooq, S; Iqbal, L & Ahmad, A. (2020). Feminine Bias: Downsizing Masculinity, Virginia Woolf's Reversal of Historical Gender Narrative in the English Fictions of Virginia Woolf" *Ilkogretim Online - Elementary Education Online*. 19 (3), 1-9.

http:// ilkogretim-online.org doi: 10.17051/ilkonline.2020.03.735355,

Singer, J. (1977). *Androgeny: Towards a New Theory of Sexuality*. Routledge & Keagan Paul.

The New Encyclopaedia Britanica: https://www.britannica.com/topic/the-arts,

The Oxford Language

Tyndall, W. Y. (1967). *The Literary Symbol*. Columbia University Press.

Woolf, V. (1927). *To the Lighthouse*, Notes: Feedbooks http://www.feedbooks.com, http://gutenberg.net.au.

Wright, E. (2022). "Re-evaluating Woolf's Androgynous Mind" https://citeseerx.ist.psu.edu/viewdoc/download?doi=10.1.1.586.5305&rep=rep1&type=pdf; 1-21

5

Re-Building Paradise
Islamic Ecosphere in Salman Rushdie's **The Satanic Verses**

MARCEL EBLIYLU NYANCHI

The events in the second half of the twentieth century have made humankind realise that modernisation and rapid population growth are ironically placing the human race on the precipice of destruction and extinction. This is because the necessities, which humanity depends on for survival and which Allah had endowed the world with freely, are degrading at a geometrical rate. According to environmental literary critics like Glotfelty and Fromm (1996), the four major parts of the environment i.e., water, earth, plants and animals which according to Islamic and Christian scriptures constitute paradise and are the source of life which humanity's greedy exploitation is ironically transforming into the source of death, especially as their destruction only estranges man from Allah or God. These environmental literary critics argue that the fact that all the world's religions preach about a paradise where the connectivity between humanity and the other species is high shows that pantheism, which constitutes an important perspective in ecocriticism can be described as a religious theory that existed since the beginning of the human race. It would therefore mean that every religious book like the Bible, the Koran, Hindu Scriptures, etc., are sourcebooks from which past, present and future ecocritics will forever tap to develop this field of human sciences. The focus of this essay is to examine the different perspectives from which Salman Rushdie's *The Satanic Verses* borrow from the Koran the different ecocritical dimensions that can encourage humankind to understand that we are an integral part of nature, which we should cherish, revere and preserve in all its magnificent beauty and diversity. As such, we should strive to live in harmony with nature locally and globally. We should thus acknowledge the inherent value of all human and non-human life and strive to treat all living beings with compassion and respect.

This perspective is critical, especially as the Koran teaches the inseparable bond between man and nature given that "from it (earth) We created you and into it. We shall send you back and from it. We will raise you a second time" (20:55). This means that in worshipping and protecting the natural environment, animals and other species, man is protecting himself and rebuilding a paradise on earth. As such, from a pantheistic perspective, the "satanic" aspect of Rushdie's *The Satanic Verses* deals with humanity's destruction of this natural cosmic harmony between humanity and other species similar to what the Romantic poet, Blake (1839) describes in "Vala/The Four Zoas." That is why the novel becomes the type of medium, which Glotfelty and Fromm (1996) describe that promotes the "exchange of ideas and information pertaining to literature that considers the relationship between human beings and the natural world" (p. xviii). Despite the religious controversies especially from Shia Muslims that have arisen because of the novel resulting in the "fatwa" on Rushdie in 1989, the novel remains an important indictment of man's catastrophic destruction of the pastoral and the ecocycle. Its two central characters, Gibreel Farishta and Saladin Chamcha, symbolise the different perspectives through which humanity is destroying while trying to preserve the ecosystem.

ALLAH'S PROMISED PARADISE

Though banned for purely religious reasons after its publication by Iranian Islamic authorities, Rushdie's The Satanic Verses has proven to be one of his major works that tries to re-establish the link between Islam and the ecocycle. From an earth-centred approach to literary studies, as proposed by Glotfelty, it can be argued that opening the novel with the explosion of an aircraft over London could be an allusion to the beginning of the world or "The Big Bang Theory," which gives a new life to its survivors. The narrator's description that:

> Out of thin air: a big bang, followed by falling stars. A universal beginning, a miniature echo of the birth of time … the jumbo jet Bostan AI-420, blew apart without any warning, high above the great, rotting, beautiful, snow-white, illuminated city, Mahagonny, Babylon, Alphaville […]. While at Himalayan heights, a brief and premature sun burst into the powdery January air (p. 4).

Rushdie's description of proper London in religious terms shows the beauty of the city that could be a reconstruction of paradise especially as the beautiful, snow-white and illuminated city shows environmental literary undertones. Given that white reflects purity, the explosion of the aircraft denotes death and rebirth, a transcendental experience, especially as Gibreel becomes an archangel while Saladin becomes Satan. This binary opposition shows the dual nature of life which could be alluded to William Blake's poem "Vala/The Four Zoas" where the description of Tharmas's fall serves as a logical starting point for the poem, especially given his role as the "parent Power" (4:7). The motifs of love, jealousy, fragmentation, and apostasy coalesce in his story. Moreover, the consequent creation of "the Circle of Destiny" (5:24) explains the origins of time and space, giving a context to the poem's action, and the violent union of the Spectre of Tharmas with Enion brings about the birth of Los and Enitharmon as the inhabitants of this fallen world of destiny. Blake paints the beginning of the world in the opening three Nights, and we see the type of paradise on earth through our spiritual activities since Allah initially built the hills, mountains and valleys as beautiful places for humanity to live in and exploit their natural resources as the *Koran* says:

> And He has made the ships to be of service unto you, that they may sail the sea by His command, and the rivers. He has made of the service unto you. And He has made the sun and the moon, constant in their courses, to be of service unto you, and He has made of service unto you the night and day. And He gives you all you seek of Him: If you would count the bounty of God, you could never reckon it (14:32-34).

The beautiful endowments that Allah has given humanity are to serve a greater purpose, the need to reconnect with the celestial paradise. Therefore, the Garden of Eden is a perfect example which literary ecocritics constantly draw from that exemplifies Allah's intended cosmic unity given that he created Adam and Eve in His image. As such, the fall of Gibreel and Saladin gives them angelic qualities because only spirits fly through the clouds and walk on the sea's surface to the shores. The fact they cannot understand how they survive the plane explosion and their safe landing from about 30,000 feet explains the existence of cosmic unity. There is a natural cohesion between the different natural forces controlled by the hidden hand of Allah, which is why Rushdie's narrator says:

> They were the only survivors of the wreck, the only ones who fell from *Bostan* and lived. They were found washed up on a beach. The more voluble of the two, the one in the purple shirt swore in his wild ramblings that they had walked upon the water, that the waves had borne them gently into shore (p. 9-10).

Here, we see the spiritual connection between Gibreel, Saladin and the sea waves as each struggles to preserve the life of the other species. In celebrating the importance of water *(maa')*, the *Koran* mentions it about 60 times, considering it the source of life for all species. The importance of water to Muslims is seen in the ritual prayer before touching the *Koran*. Equally, to go around the Ka'bah in Mecca, the Muslim must be ritually pure by making ritual ablutions with water. To them, water symbolises knowledge and faith because in it, there are spirits that guide those who use it. That is why according to ancient ecocritics, the destruction of any natural habitat like water needed rituals to be carried out to appease the water spirits as White (1996, p. 10) highlights that:

> In antiquity every tree, every spring, every stream, every hill had its own *genius loci*, its guardian spirit. These spirits were accessible to men, but were very unlike men; centaurs, fauns, and mermaids show their ambivalence. Before one cut a tree, mined a mountain, or dammed a brook, it was important to placate the spirit in charge of that particular situation, and to keep it placated.

The wanton destruction of forests and land reclamation projects only justify that humans no longer appease the spirits that live in these sacred places. To show the importance of the natural environment, Gibreel builds his house on top of Malabar Hill which is on the highest ground in the city, so that he can get a panoramic view of the latter across the sea. This brings him in constant touch with the natural breeze from the sea that is free from contamination by industrialisation in the city below. The fact that he names his home Everest Villa, an allusion to Mount Everest, which is the highest in the world and an important tourist attraction, shows his love for extraordinary natural beauty. From this height, Gibreel believes himself to be a servant of Allah, which is why he dreams of taking the place of the Prophet in the *Koran* who makes a great "success of his job as the business manager of the wealthy widow, Khadija, and ended up marrying her as well" (p. 22). These fantasies only confirm that Allah can make any man His servant and Gibreel's major task as a prophet is to re-establish the broken bond between humankind, the natural environment, and all the other species.

Rushdie further celebrates environmental consciousness through Henry and Rosa Diamond whose love for nature and animals surprises their friends and neighbours. At first, Rosa is shocked upon noticing that her husband loves animals more than her. The narrator opines that Henry's love:

> Was reserved for birds. Marsh hawks, screamers, snipe. In a small rowing boat on the local lagunas he spent his happiest days amid the bulrushes with his field-glasses to his eyes. Once on the train to Buenos Aires he embarrassed Rosa by demonstrating his favourite birdcalls in the dinning-car, cupping his hands around his mouth: sleepyhead bird, vanduria ibis, trupial [...]. At night, she took to walking out into the pampa and lying on her back to look at the galaxy above (p. 146).

The activities of Henry and Rosa Diamond concur with the desires of ecocritics because they successfully maintain and protect the relationship between humans and animals. Rushdie's crusade here is to create awareness about the importance of this connectivity, which is a step towards rebuilding another paradise on earth, a perspective that his detractors think is not very important. Henry's ecological consciousness could be likened to that of Saint Francis of Assisi whom they saw as a radical Catholic priest because he preached to animals when the people refused to listen to him on grounds that he was mad. Describing the attempts made by Saint Francis to convert animals and birds, White (1996, p. 13) further says:

> Later commentators have said that Francis preached to the birds as a rebuke to men who would not listen. The records do not read so: he urged the little birds to praise God, and in spiritual ecstasy, they flapped their wings and chirped rejoicing [...]. The land around Gubbio in the Aprennines was being ravaged by a fierce wolf. Saint Francis, says the legend, talked to the wolf and persuaded him of the error of his ways. The wolf repented, died in the odour of sanctity, and was buried in consecrated ground.

Saint Francis's crusade, according to Glotfelty and Fromm is one of the greatest moves in the history of ecocriticism especially because those who struggle to preserve their environment and animals are in most cases seen as mad people by their societies. Similarly, when Gibreel recovers from a mysterious illness, he starts behaving abnormally. The narrator says from the hospital, he drives directly to the Taj Hotel and falls hungrily on the food in the:

> Great dining room with its buffet table groaning under the weight of forbidden food, and he loaded his plate with all of it, the pork sausages from Wiltshire and the cured York hams and the rashers of bacon from god knows where; with the gammon steaks of his unbelief and the pig's trotters of secularism; and then, standing there in the middle of the hall, while photographers popped up from nowhere, he began to eat as fast as possible (p. 29-30).

The spirit of Rekha that saves Gibreel also opens his eyes to the importance of the consumption of all the species in the natural environment. Gibreel's blasphemy is the talk of the town because, according to Islamic teachings, the pig is a dirty animal that true Muslims should not consume. That is why people are surprised to see a Muslim like Gibreel consuming pork publicly, a thing he never did all his life before the illness. Arguably, the illness is his transcendental period to attain some spiritual momentum geared towards the protection and consumption of all the species created by Allah. According to literary ecocritics, some religious doctrines are a failure because they forbid the eating of species created by Allah, thereby disobeying Allah who created food, plants, and animals to constitute the sustenance of human life on earth as the *Koran* puts it:

> Then let man consider his nourishment: that we pour down the rain in showers, and we split the earth in fragments, and therein make the grain to grow, and vines and herbs, and olives and palms, and gardens of dense foliage, and fruits and fodder – provision for you and your cattle (80: 24-32).

From the above, the question remains as to why would humans till the earth and plant crops to feed animals like pigs that eventually cannot be consumed because of some religious belief. Rushdie's description of Gibreel's activity in the Taj Hotel has largely garnered criticism from Muslims who think it is taboo to eat pork. Ironically, Rushdie, by this presentation confirms that to engage in the crusade to foster ecocriticism implies coming up against a number of socio-cultural and religious laws.

From another perspective, the novelist looks at the notion of paradise from man's relationship with insects and plants. In his opinion, spirituality transcends natural human reasoning, which is why the people of Jahilia do not understand why the old woman, Bibiji, is able to communicate with butterflies and plants. The fact that she lives for over two hundred and forty-two years could be because of her wisdom to interact with both plants, insects and animals, the reason why she is described as a legend because her:

> Grave until its location was forgotten, had the property of curing impotence and warts. Since the death of Bibiji one hundred and twenty years ago, the butterflies had vanished into the same realm of the legendary as Bibiji herself, so that when they came back exactly one hundred and one years after their departure, it looked at first, like an omen of some imminent, wonderful thing (p. 217)

From a literary ecocritical perspective, we realise that because of her spirituality, her grave becomes an important tourist site and a paradise because the grass and earth on her grave have the capacity to treat impotence and warts. Her death becomes a return to the natural elements, and she gets a new form of "afterlife" because her actions, ideas and memories live on. Over the years, humans' wanton destruction of the ecocycle has, in the context of the text, caused these spiritual endowments on Bibiji's grave to disappear, which is why the reappearance of these butterflies one century later only rekindles the hopes of the inhabitants of the coming of a second prophetess. This time, it is the prophetess Ayesha who comes with a message from Allah to convey to the people of Jahilia and Titlipur to go to Mecca where they would kiss the black stone in the sacred mosque and be forgiven of their sins as they enter paradise. That is why many respect Ayesha because they had seen the importance of the grass on Bibiji's grave and the miracles performed by her butterflies. This resonates with Manes' (1996, p. 15) views that:

> Those that see the natural world as inspirited, not just people, but also animals, plants, and even "inert" entities such as stones and rivers are perceived as being articulate and at times intelligible subjects, able to communicate and interact with humans for good or ill. In addition to human language, there is also the language of birds, the wind, earthworms, wolves, and waterfalls – a world of autonomous speakers whose intents […] one ignores at one's peril.

To Manes, it is due to the intricate link between man and the other species that in paradise, Allah speaks to the people through plants and animals. Consequently, to continue to enjoy such divine blessing, ecocritics encourage people to preserve their natural resources, protect animals and plants, improve and develop the environment. That is why Ayesha protects and manipulates the mystical butterflies in *The Satanic Verses* in a way that astounds the Titlipurians. The protective nature of these butterflies whenever there is an imminent danger simply builds spiritual momentum in the Muslims who follow her to Mecca. Ironically, despite evidence that the natural environment and other species are indispensable in the survival of the human race, man's activities continue to degrade his environment and the ecocycle, thereby estranging him from paradise. *The Satanic Verses* become a plea for the protection of the environment because in it, there is abundance to sustain human life.

THE JAHILIYYA AND NATURE DESTRUCTION

Protecting the environment is an act that has both natural and spiritual advantages. In the text I analyse here, the author satirises the destruction of the natural environment because the inhabitants of Jahilia do not understand the importance of preserving their environment to accommodate other natural species. That is why he names the town Jahilia, a metaphor for the pre-Islamic period called the "jahiliyya." According to Berkey (2003, p. 39):

> Muslims refer to the pre-Islamic period as the *jahiliyya*, the "time of ignorance" before the coming of the Koranic revelation. From a historical rather than a theological viewpoint, the term is an apt one, although for entirely different reasons.

In this regard, Rushdie's Prophet Mahound introduces the *Koran* to Jahilians encouraging them to develop their natural environments to contain other species especially because the city is entirely on sand in the desert. It is a city of nomads, who, according to the writer, settled there some four generations before the coming of the prophet of Islam. However, it is ironical that the people persecute all those who spill the little water they have on the ground. The narrator says:

> Water is the enemy in Jahilia. Carried in earthen pots, it must never be spilled (the penal code deals fiercely with offenders), for where it drops the city erodes alarmingly. Holes appear in roads, houses tilt and sway [...]. It never rains in Jahilia; there are no fountains in the silicon gardens. A few palms stand in enclosed courtyards, their roots travelling far and wide below the earth in search of moisture (p. 94).

The only water source in the city is from springs that the people use for their daily activities. When Mahound discovers the harsh laws on those who spill water, he encourages them to water their environment and plant more trees and flowers. This is because the dryness only adds to the environmental problems they already have. Given that, the city is strictly a commercial area; Jahilians are more involved in activities that will generate wealth. They do not develop their environment, and Mahound's presence reminds them that they have wasted much time chasing earthly pleasures. Arguably, Rushdie's position here is that Jahilia has an environmental crisis similar to what Rueckert (1996, p. 116) says to Barry Commoner that:

> We are in an environmental crisis because the means by which we use the ecosphere to produce wealth are destructive of the ecosystem itself. The

present system of production is self-destructive. The present course of human civilisation is suicidal. In our unwitting march toward ecological suicide we have run out of options. Human beings have broken out of the circle of life, driven not by biological needs, but by social organisation which they have devised to conquer nature.

Here, Commoner is more concerned with how man estranges himself from nature for selfish reasons. Jahilians completely neglect the importance of their natural environment in the daily survival of their community and are more interested in trading activities. That is why when Mahound receives the calling to form Islam and evangelise his fellow Jahilians, he preaches to them about the connectivity of everything in life and that water spilling should not be treasonable as the laws stipulate. This is because Muslims need water for ablution during prayers to praise Allah given that the *Koran* emphasises the importance of water through the following question: "have you considered, if your water were one morning have seeped away, who then could bring you clear-flowing water?" (67:30). This verse educates Jahilians that water comes from Allah and they should not prohibit their citizens from spilling because it only moisturises the soil for the survival of other species.

The absence of faith in Jahilia is alluded to the environmental degradation that troubles Mahound who foresees an apocalypse of an unimaginable magnitude. Rushdie brings in the archangel Gibreel to guide both Mahound and Ayesha who are the pillars of Islam in the novel. Given that Jahilians neglect their environment and do not listen to the voice of Allah through Mahound and Ayesha, angel Gibreel dreams of Allah's punishment to Jahilians as the narrator says:

> Gibreel dreamed a drought; the land browned under the rainless skies. The corpses of buses and ancient monuments rotting in the fields beside the crops [...] the wild donkeys fucking wearily and dropping dead, while still conjoined, in the middle of the road, the trees standing on roots exposed by soil erosion and looking like huge wooden claws scrabbling for water in the earth, the destitute farmers being obliged to work for the state as manual labourers, digging a reservoir by the truck road, an empty container for rain that wouldn't fall (p. 479).

This is the dream that Gibreel dreams and which is further manifested in the experiences of Mirza Saeed Akhtar, the rich landowner who does not care about the poor in his society. People like Mirza who exploit the poor and

Jahilia's natural resources govern Jahilia. As a corrupt landowner, and during the pilgrimage to Mecca, he tries to dissuade Ayesha and other pilgrims from their spiritual journey. According to Ayesha, the prolonged drought and starvation symbolise Allah's wrath upon the community who punishes them with environmental hazards. The *Koran* condemns people like Mirza that "when he turns away, he hastens through the land to cause corruption therein and to destroy the crops and cattle. And God loves not corruption" (2:205).

That is why Mirza remains ashore by the sea because he lacks faith in the pilgrimage and cannot walk the bottom of the sea like the believers. Consequently, he returns to Jahilia, which Rushdie now calls "Peristan" as a metaphor for a city that has perished in the eyes of Allah. Here, there are very few humans left because everything is dead, with vultures eating up the remaining corpses of the unbelievers. The earth in Jahilia is scourged and infertile because "the village had crumbled into dust; landless peasants and looters had tried to seize the abandoned land, but the drought had driven them away. There had been no rain here" (p. 506). Mirza's greed is his flaw, which contributes immensely in the death of Jahilia's ecocycle if one goes by Meeker's (1996, p. 162) observation that:

> No human has ever known what it means to live in a climax ecosystem, at least not since the emergence of consciousness, which has made us human. We have generally acted the role of the pioneer species, dedicating ourselves to survival through the destruction of all our competitors and to achieving effective dominance over other forms of lice.

Rushdie, in this novel like Meeker, condemns the selfish activities of the rich whose wealth blinds them from the vision of paradise. They have transformed the world into a barren landscape because it is now void of morality and the road to heaven becomes thorny and rough. Rushdie thus fictionalises the world to be the wilderness between Jahilia and Mount Cone where Archangel Gibreel sits and waits for the true believers to come and meet him. This symbolism comes out as the narrator describes the barren land that:

> To reach Mount Cone from Jahilia one must walk into dark ravines where the sand is not white, not the pure sand filtered long ago through the bodies of sea-cucumbers, but black and dour, sucking light from the sun? Coney crouches over you like an imaginary beast. You ascend along its spine. Leaving behind the trees, white-flowered with thick, milky leaves, you climb the last trees among the boulders, which get larger as you get higher, until they resemble huge walls and start blotting out the sun. The lizards are blue as

shadows. Then you are on the peak, Jahilia behind you, the featureless desert ahead. You descend on the desert side, and about five hundred feet down you reach the cave, which is high enough to stand upright in, and whose floor is covered in miraculous albino sand. As you climb you hear the desert doves calling your name, and the rocks greet you, too, in your own language, crying Mahound, Mahound. When you reach the cave you are tired, you lie down, you fall asleep (p. 109-110).

Therefore, from Jahilia to Mount Cone, Muslims pass through a symbolic wilderness before getting to paradise. Mahound passes through this wilderness to get to Archangel Gibreel for revelations that he needs to communicate to Muslims. If the road to Mount Cone symbolises the wilderness, it is because of human activities which are irreligious and which have tended to impact the ecocycle. That is why literary ecocritics like Norman and Kraft (1994) argue that something needs to be done quickly. They point out that "by intervening before an ecosystem becomes so degraded that few options are left, this approach facilitates carefully planned trade-offs between environmental protection and economic growth and thus supports the goal of sustainable development" (p. 380). Thus, according to Rushdie's *The Satanic Verses*, man needs to reconnect with his environment because in it lays the potential to communicate with the spiritual realm.

REBUILDING NATURE AND ISLAMIC SPIRITUALITY

In this section, we shall examine the different perspectives from which *The Satanic Verses* valorises the protection of the bond between man, nature and all the other species. Given man's wanton destruction of the ecocycle, Islam, as a religion, continues to advocate the planting and preservation of trees, which is now a culture in Kashmir. Rushdie's narrator tells us that in Kashmir, a child's life is synonymous with a tree because when he is born, a walnut tree is planted. The narrator describes this symbolic event about Saladin when he returns to his father's house and sees his childhood tree still standing:

> When he saw the walnut tree in which his father had claimed that his soul was kept, his hand began to shake [...]. In Kashmir, he told Zeeny, your birth-tree is a financial investment of a sort. When it comes of age, the grown walnut is comparable to a matured insurance policy; it is a valuable tree, it can be sold, to pay for weddings, or to start in life (p. 65).

The importance of this tree transcends sociocultural paradigms because it has a spiritual significance. The fact that a tree is a microcosm of a child's life obliges the family to protect such a tree against destruction, just as they will protect their child's life. Saladin is touched spiritually when he sees his forty-year-old walnut tree because in it lays his entire life. The spiritual importance of this tree could be likened to that in James Cameron's *Avatar* where the tree in the world of Pandora serves as the abode of the goddess Egwa and the source of power for the animals and people in that society. Rushdie's narrator further makes us to understand that in Kashmiri society, the planting of walnut trees encourages high birth rates because since each new-born child symbolises a new tree, the notion of forestation becomes imperative and the cutting down of walnut trees has both socio-cultural and religious consequences. This idea is important in the discourse of literary ecocriticism as such trees reflect the goodness of its species as Manes (1996, p. 20) further opines:

> The goodness of the species transcends the goodness of the individual, as form transcends matter; therefore the multiplication of species is a greater addition to the good of the universe than the multiplication of individuals of a single species. The perfection of the universe therefore requires not only a multitude of individuals, but also diverse kinds, and therefore diverse grades of things.

Accordingly, rapid population explosion without an increase in plants and crops to feed this population is detrimental to the human species because there will be food shortages and no trees to purify the air we breathe. This is important because even in Islamic mythology, the Prophet recommended planting trees and urged people to protect them to the extent that planting a tree was considered an act of worship, for which special prayer was recommended. The Holy Prophet's eco-consciousness is seen when he instructed before battle that his soldiers should not harm women, children, the elderly, and those who surrendered and not to destroy or burn farms and gardens. In his opinion, his jihads were to convert the pagan tribes and not deprive them of food and shelter because he knew they still needed to continue surviving after their conversion.

The importance given to the walnut tree in Kashmir is similar to the importance of spices in Indian history. Rushdie's *The Satanic Verses* traces the reasons for the discovery of India to the region's abundance in spices that set Vasco da Gama and his tall ships to the Far East. He continues this historicity in another novel, *The Moor's Last Sigh*, where the narrator reminisces about India's pastoral beauty:

> I repeat: the pepper, if you please; for if it had not been for peppercorns, then what is ending now in East and West might never have begun. Pepper it was that brought Vasco da Gama's tall ships across the ocean, from Lisbon's Tower of Belem to the Malabar Coast: first to Calicut and later, for its lagoon harbour, to Cochin. English and French sailed in the wake of that first-arrived Portugee, so that in the period called Discovery-of India (p. 4).

Before da Gama discovered India, the region had been Islamised by the followers of Mohammad. The spices and the environmental beauty that da Gama meets and appreciates are a manifestation of the people's adherence to the religious teachings of the Prophet. Ironically, we can argue that the discovery of India brought ecological damage to this fine environment because trading companies exploited and exported these spices to the West, which now disconnects the people's culture from their environment. This is where Glotfelty (1996, p. xix) comes in with her definition of literary ecocriticism as a theory of reconnection that:

> All ecological criticism shares the fundamental premise that human culture is connected to the physical world, affecting it and affected by it. Ecocriticism takes as its subject the interconnections between nature and culture, specifically the cultural artefacts of language and literature. As a critical stance, it has one foot in literature and the other on land; as a theoretical discourse, it negotiates between the human and the nonhuman.

This interconnection is important for the survival of the human race because man depends on other species and elements to exist. Proof of this is the spring of Zamzam in Islamic mythology where Archangel Gibreel guides Hagar and Ismail after Ibrahim rejects them:

> In ancient times, the patriarch Ibrahim came into this valley with Hagar and Ismail, their son. Here, in this waterless wilderness, he abandoned her. She asked him, can this be God's will? He replied, it is, and left the bastard [...]. Hagar wasn't a witch. She was trusting: then surely He will not let me perish. After Ibrahim left her, she fed the baby at her breast until her milk ran out. Then she climbed two hills, first Safa then Marwah, running from one to the other in her desperation, trying to sight a tent, a camel, a human being. She saw nothing. That was when He came to her, Gibreel, and showed her the waters of Zamzam. So Hagar survived (p. 95).

Since Archangel Gibreel saved them, pilgrims now visit Mounts Safa and

Marwah to pay tributes to the woman the Archangel vindicates. Here again we see the link between the environment and spirituality because it is Hagar's trust in Allah that saves them after their excommunication which justifies what the *Koran* says that water can appear anywhere if there is faith in Allah "Have We not made the earth a vessel to hold the living and the dead? And we have made in it lofty mountains and provided you with sweet water to drink" (77:22-27). That is why Muslims continue to visit Safa, Marwah and Zamzam during pilgrimages. These sacred places symbolise an Islamic paradise on earth, which Rushdie describes as having the perfume of balsam, cassia, cinnamon, frankincense, etc. (p. 95). That is why every true Muslim has to visit it at least once in his lifetime.

Moreover, Rushdie celebrates the importance of the environment through Allie Cone, the world champion in mountain climbing who has earned the name as the "Ice Queen" of the Himalaya and the Everest mountains or the "Golden girl from the roof of the world" (p. 308-309). Through Cone, a certain degree of spirituality comes to bare especially as she sees the face of Allah on the mountains as she tells her friends:

> I believe it all: that the universe has a sound, that you can lift a veil and see the face of God, everything. I saw the Himalayas stretching below me and that was God's face too […]. Then the visions began, the rainbows looping and dancing in the sky, the radiance pouring down like the waterfall from the sun, and there were angels (p. 198-199).

These beautiful scenes seen from very high above symbolise the wonders of Allah. In Rushdie's opinion, Cone feels she is in paradise because the world down is completely different. In her opinion, one needs to go very high up to understand that Allah is miraculous in the way He designed the world to communicate with him. Manes (1996, p. 20) further opines, "exegesis established God as a transcendental subject speaking through natural entities, which, like words on a page, had a symbolic meaning, but no autonomous voice." To observe these natural entities, you need to get very high up which justifies why Muslims believe that Allah and the beautiful Shalimar gardens are high up there. For this reason, Cone in that height believes the mountains are a blessed place to observe the world since the *Koran* says "and He has set within it mountains standing firm, and blessed it, and ordained in it its diverse sustenance in four days, alike for all that seek" (41:10). The natural beauty of the world seen from above can equally be alluded to the notion of the ascension of Moses to the hill to get his commandments or that of Christ and Mary in

Christian mythology after their deaths.

Rushdie's ecocritical stance is highlighted through Ayesha's spirituality in *The Satanic Verses*. The fact that when she returns from the hill after praying to Allah and tells the people of Jahilia that Allah has commanded that they should go on a pilgrimage to Mecca without fear of opposition is because she is guided by forces that exist in her environment. That is why when armed miners of Sarang on the road to Mecca who want to sabotage this spiritual journey attack them, Allah sends down a storm to protect the pilgrims. The narrator says the miners block:

> The pilgrims' routes with dead bicycles and waited behind this barricade of broken wheels, bent handlebars and silenced bells as the Ayesha Haj entered the northern sector of the street. Ayesha walked towards the mob as if it did not exist and when she reached the crossroads, beyond which the clubs and knives of the enemy awaited her, there was a thunderclap like trumpet of doom and an ocean fell down out of the sky [...]. But now the rainstorm redoubled its force, and then doubled it again, falling from the sky in thick slabs through which it was getting difficult to breathe, as though the earth was being engulfed, and the firmament above were reuniting with the firmament below (p. 490-491).

The storm that kills the protesters is a demonstration of Allah's wrath, which symbolises an endless sea falling from the sky, and this action increases the faith pilgrims have for Allah. This justifies Koranic teachings that in times of great need, "He caused rain to descend on you from heaven to cleanse you therewith" (8:11). Furthermore, the fact that Ayesha's spiritual butterflies regroup all the scattered pilgrims into one flock, healing pilgrims who are wounded in their frantic attempts to "escape from the storm or pilgrims who drown and even die in the storm are resuscitated by these butterflies" (p. 495) celebrates the importance of other species in the survival of humankind. Examining the spiritual powers of these butterflies, Stephanie (2005) says "having left the pilgrims during an almost supernaturally violent storm, the butterflies reappear to gather and lead the pilgrims back together" (p. 264). Significantly, the storm disperses the pilgrims, whereas the protesters drown in the flood.

Furthermore, the belief in Allah helps the pilgrims traverse the wilderness of sin, symbolised by the land's barren nature until they get to the sea whose vastness and beauty symbolise the abode of Allah. Here, Ayesha's faith is once again alluded to that of Moses when we examine eyewitness reports of Allah's mysterious opening of the Arabian Sea for Ayesha and the pilgrims to go to

Mecca as Mohammad Din explains:

> I saw it with my own eyes; I saw the sea divide, like hair being combed; and they were all there, far away, walking away from me. She was there also, my wife, Khadija, whom I love. This is what Osman the bullock-boy told the detectives, who had been badly shaken by the Sarpanch's disposition: 'at first I was in great fear of drowning myself. Still, I was searching, searching, mainly for her, Ayesha, whom I knew from before her alteration. And just at the last, I saw it happen, the marvellous thing. The water opened, and I saw them go along the ocean floor, among the dying fish.' Sri Srinivas, too, swore by the goddess Lakshmi that he had seen the parting of the Arabian Sea (p. 504).

Ayesha is likened to Moses in the *Bible* when she and the pilgrims walk the beautiful bottom of the Arabian Sea and arrive in Mecca meanwhile those who do not believe in the pilgrimage are disappointed at the end. This is evident when Sri Srinivas tells his friends that it is a shame that their lack of faith in Allah has made Him close the waters that symbolise the gates of paradise on their faces. Thus, the ocean becomes a transcendental signifier of paradise and which is why ecocritics continue to advocate that we protect the seas and all the creatures that live in it as Rueckert (1996, p. 107) notes that:

> The problem now as most ecologists agree, is to find ways of keeping the human community from destroying the natural community, and with it the human community. This is what ecologists like to call the self-destructive or suicidal motive that is inherent in our prevailing and paradoxical attitude toward nature. The conceptual and practical problem is to find the grounds upon which the two communities – the human, the natural – can coexist, co-operate, and flourish in the biosphere.

From the perspective above, it stands to reason that the best way to attain such organic unity is to accept that there is an interconnectivity of all things regarding Islamic spirituality. Rushdie follows these lines of argument in *The Satanic Verses*, as shown by my analysis. From the ecocritical perspective, it can be concluded that the natural environment has proven to be the abode of Allah, and if one were to enjoy this paradise, one needs to protect all the species that exist on earth because Allah created us to cohabit and ensure each other's survival.

CONCLUSION

Given that humankind will always continue to inhabit the earth, attending to issues of the environment remains primordial because humankind's survival depends on how the natural environment is managed. The benefits that one takes from the environment are not limited to material or physical. They also include mental and psychological benefits if we agree that Allah created the earth in the image of paradise or the Shalimar gardens. Therefore, one is bound to preserve the elements of the earth because every Muslim in his ritual prayer has to prostrate to Allah several times on the earth or an earthly material like soil or sand. Furthermore, if water is not available, or using water is harmful to one's health (e.g., because of injury), one needs to use earth or earthly materials in a special way to perform ritual ablution since the *Koran* says, "and among His signs is that He has created you from dust; then behold, you are humans scattered widely" (30:20). Thus, the environment and the species that inhabit it are all and will return to dust, meaning that the environment is indispensable in our survival, and we need to protect it because we are part of it. That is why it becomes incumbent on everyone to advocate the protection of the environment from every perspective, as my analysis of Rushdie's novel has shown.

REFERENCES

Berkey, P. J. (2003). *The Formation of Islam: Religion and Society in the Near East, 600–1800*. Cambridge University Press.

Blake, W. (1839). *Vala/The Four Zoas*. Oxford University Press.

Cameron J, Per. Worthington, S., Saldana, Z., Alonso, L., Rodriguez, M., (2014). Twentieth Century Fox.

Dawood, N.J. (Trans). (1956). *Koran*. Penguin Books.

Glotfelty, C. (1996). Introduction: Literary Studies in an Age of Environmental Crises. *The Ecocriticism Reader: Landmarks in Literary Ecology*. University of Georgia Press.

Glotfelty, C. & Fromm, H. (Eds.), (1996). *The Ecocriticism Reader: Landmarks in Literary Ecology*. University of Georgia Press.

Love, A. G. (1996). Revaluing Nature: Toward an Ecological Criticism. In C. Glotfelty, C. & H. Fromm. (Eds.), *The Ecocriticism Reader: Landmarks in Literary Ecology*. (pp. 225-240). University of Georgia Press.

Manes, C. (1996). Nature and Silence. In C. Glotfelty, C. & H. Fromm. (Eds.), *The Ecocriticism Reader: Landmarks in Literary Ecology*. (pp.15-29). University of Georgia Press.

Meeker, W. J. (1996). The Comic Mode. In C. Glotfelty, C. & H. Fromm. (Eds.), *The Ecocriticism Reader: Landmarks in Literary Ecology*. (pp.155-169). University of

Georgia Press.

Rueckert, W. (1996). Literature and Ecology: An Experiment in Ecocriticism. In C. Glotfelty, C. & H. Fromm. (Eds.), *The Ecocriticism Reader: Landmarks in Literary Ecology.* (pp. 105-123). University of Georgia Press.

Rushdie, S. (1988). *The Satanic Verses.* Penguin Group.

Rushdie, S. (1995). *The Moor's Last Sigh.* Random.

Sampson, J. (Ed), (1913). *The Poetical Works of William Blake.* Oxford University Press.

Stephanie, J. (2005). Of Numerology and Butterflies: Magical Realism in Salman Rushdie's *The Satanic Verses. A Companion to Magical Realism.* Eds. Stephen M. Hart and Wen-chin Ouyang. (pp. 256-66). Athenaeum Press

Norman, J. V. & Kraft, E.M. (Eds.), (1994). *Environmental Policy in the 1990s: Toward a New Agenda.* Congressional Quarterly.

White, L. J. (1996). The Historical Roots of Our Ecologic Crises. In C. Glotfelty, C. & H. Fromm. (Eds.), *The Ecocriticism Reader: Landmarks in Literary Ecology.* (pp. 03-14). University of Georgia Press.

Part Two

Language, Conflict Creation and Conflict Resolution

6

Insults and Spear Words in Music
Cameroon Pidgincreole as a Shield

HANS MBONWUH FONKA

Cameroon Pidgincreole (Henceforth CPc,) an appellation used to replace Cameroon Pidgin English (Fonka, 2019), is an accommodating language in Cameroon in that almost everybody can claims to be a speaker, the degree of use notwithstanding. Because of the multiplicity of its speakers, it has had a wide variety of functions over the years (Mbangwana, 2004; Fonka, 2014a). Although conflict cannot be considered one of the functions of CPc or any other language, conflict cannot exist in the absence of language. CPc is used to create or resolve conflict, especially in music. It is also used to resolve political conflicts, as with the Anglophone crisis in Cameroon (Fonka, 2022). When conflicts occur, things fall apart, turn, transform themselves, and come together in new ways (Cloke, 2001). Political conflicts are the major types of conflicts we have in the world today. Conflicts usually do not start with using arms; they start with ideological differences that eventually get verbalised. These exchanges may be mediated or direct. Arms are only employed when language fails to provide a solution. Words can induce pain and death more than missiles, as they hardly miss their target. Different people are gifted with varied speech abilities to handle social, political and economic issues amongst others. Given that speech is interpreted asymmetrically from one receiver to the other, what some people receive with joy can just be a deadly weapon to others.

Language produces conflict not only because the target's heart is unjustly pierced by the speaker with spear words but also because how that issue is addressed is considered derogatory by the person addressed. Leaders expect complete submission and trust from their followers. Anyone who expresses open dissatisfaction is not often considered a loyal follower. It is said that "all conflicts and complaints are the results of someone's expectations not being met" (MTD Training, 2010, p. 11). This is especially true when expectations are repeatedly heightened with promises of a better situation and little or nothing is done to fulfil such promises. Citizens, therefore, tend to use spear words against their leaders when some of these promises have not been met. As Cloke (2001, p. 4) indicates, every honest communication poses a risk that we will hear something that could challenge or change us. Change, in itself, is perceived differently by different people. When leaders fail to meet the expectations of their followers, the latter consider this a change of attitude. When followers speak against leaders, the former ties this to insubordination and disrespect of hierarchy, thus creating a change of attitude as well. Cloke (2001, p. 4) sustains this argument by asserting that "all significant change, whether in how organisations are structured or who makes family decisions or how we live our lives, will be perceived as dangerous because we do not and cannot fully understand where it will lead."

Over the years, language has been used as a battle sword and a shield that individuals and communities employ against each other. In Cameroon, CPc in particular, has been used for insults and spear words by various persons in different situations to induce pain while at the same time to shield attacks. This paper examines insults and spear words used in CPc by musicians like Lapiro de Mbanga. It holds that when language targets personalities and not structures, conflict is bound to occur. This paper attempts to bring out the insults and spear words used in CPc against some personalities and the conflict it brings. It equally attempts to determine whether the CPc (Mboko variety) variety can function as a shield against counterattacks. This paper employs the Social Conflict Theory by Karl Marx as its analytical framework.

DEFINITION OF KEYWORDS

I have provided definitions of some concepts used in this work for clarity. These definitions, which include Cameroon Pidgincreole, Insults and spear words, have been drawn from linguistic sources and various dictionaries.

Cameroon Pidgincreole (CPc)

Cameroon Pidgincreole (CPc) is a term coined and adopted for Cameroon Pidgin English by Fonka (2011, 2019) based on its evolution. CPc, according to this source, is no longer a pidgin because it is continuously being used for many other purposes other than trade, the main reason for its creation and is now the mother tongue of some Cameroonians. These mother tongue speakers of pidgin do not constitute any agglomeration to be considered creole speakers. As the doted mother tongue speakers increase daily, it is hoped that CPc will become a creole. This language has grown into varieties used by the communities within which those varieties have grown. Some variations are engendered by geographical distances separating the speakers (the northwest and the southwest varieties, for example), while others are based on social classification, such as the Mboko variety. Some are understood across the board, while others are understood only by the group that speaks it. The case of the group-specific variety is the Mboko variety that Lapiro de Mbanga uses in his songs. This is the variety that is examined in this paper.

Insult

According to the Cambridge Advanced Learner's Dictionary (3rd ed.), an insult is an offensive remark or action. To insult is to say or do something to someone rude or offensive. In almost similar but more emphatic terms, Random House Webster's College Dictionary defines insult as "a deliberately discourteous or rude remark or act that humiliates, wounds the feeling, and arouses anger." Not recognising a person's authority simply in action, even if you lack the courage to say it to his/her face, is an insult. Insults directed at individuals, especially those holding public offices, are, depending on the circumstance, considered an insult to that office. This explains why insults to individuals sometimes provoke public action. According to Neu (2008), Etymologists trace the word insult to the Latin *salıre* (to leap) and its frequentative form *saltare, saltus* a leap, *insultare* to leap upon (also translated as jump or trample on, which is close to the early meaning of insult as exult or act arrogantly). Neu (2008, p. 8) further says that insult involves at least two states of mind: the insulter and the insulted, or the would-be insulter and the might-be insulted. The question we may want to answer in this paper is whether it can still be considered an insult even if what is said, though-provoking anger, is true.

Spear words

Spear words, on their part, are such words that are considered hurting and which shock and offend the ears of polite society. Spear words are contextual because what one society considers bad language may be normal usage in another. In other words, curse words are culturally and morally relative and vary in potency from person to person. When words are sent out to pierce an opponent, the response in most cases is always disastrous because, in some cases, they are responded to with violent action, which, in some cases, has ended up in death.

LITERATURE REVIEW

In the use of Cameroon Pidgincreole, different domains of use encounter different types of conflicts. Though the domain of education has always been in the lead, this chapter handles the conflict hidden in the entertainment domain. The following sections examine the use of CPc in Cameroon and the conflict areas.

The use of CPc in Cameroon

Scholarship on Cameroon Pidgincreole cannot be over-emphasised because many have researched and published on this topic. We will examine the use of CPc in Cameroon in just a few domains related to the present study. These will include education and entertainment because music is both for education and entertainment.

CPc for Education in Cameroon

Concerning the use of CPc in education in Cameroon, many misconceptions have been raised over the years about its destructive role in the study of the English language. This position has been publicised by the mass media that uses CPc to run some programmes. It should be made clear that currently, CPc is not the language of education anywhere in Cameroon, at least officially. Nevertheless, this language is used by some teachers in the English-speaking part of Cameroon to make their lessons understood by their pupils (Mbangwana, 1983). Given that it is the most widespread language of interaction in Cameroon and the primary language to many children residing in the two English-speaking regions in Cameroon - the Northwest and the Southwest regions, it can be an advantaged language of education than any other one (Neba et al., 2006; Atechi, 2011; Atechi & Fonka, 2007; Fonka, 2011, 2014a). In many formal educational establishments, CPc is banned, though not officially (Alobwede, 1998; Simo Bobda, 2001; Sala, 2006, 2009; Chia, 2009; Fonka, 2011; Atechi, 2011) to improve the correct use of the English language. However, the question that needs an answer is whether this ban has caused any improvement in English in Cameroon. The answer to this question is partly answered by Fonka (2014b) when he observes that there is a decline in the use of spoken English on Anglophone campuses in the Francophone regions of Cameroon. As he states, one of the reasons for this fall is that the linguistic situation in Anglophone schools, which used to be highly CPc and then English language, is now French, English and CPc. According to this study, the primary rival language on these campuses is French and not CPc. One would have expected the English language to improve with the decline in the use of CPc on campus; instead, the contrary is true. This means the fight to kill CPc is a vain venture because nothing positive promises to come out of it. This equally means that if a concurrent language causes a fall in the standard of English in Cameroon, it is certainly not the sole responsibility of CPc.

Despite the above argument indicating the strength of CPc and the apparent impossibility of its being destructive as claimed even by its speakers, Ngefac and Sala (2006) express surprise at the fact that some people are still very sluggish to accept and promote it as the language of official transaction. Education is one of such official domains, as seen with their reference to Kouega (2001), where only a handful of the informants (29.6%) favoured the idea that Pidgin as a medium of instruction in the early years of primary school could facilitate understanding in the teaching of science subjects. To further prove that people simply claim to reject CPc but their actions do the contrary, Chia (2009), in an intelligent observation, found that students discuss science subjects in pidgin at the University of Buea. The same observation Simo Bobda (2009) had for the University of Yaounde I. This leads this author to assert, along with the preceding authors that in Cameroon, CPc is used unofficially in official milieus.

Though CPc is not used formally as indicated, it is a highly informal language of education with no restrictions on its usage. Publicity, for example, is an informal type of education wherein people are drilled on the merits of a new product or service in the market. This is one of the biggest domains in which CPc is used to introduce new products to Cameroonians and to educate them on their use. Ayafor (2005) indicates that Cameroon Pidgin is now one of the broadcasting languages, especially on radio and television. It should be noted that many informal educational programmes are broadcast on the radio and television in CPc.

CPc for Music in Cameroon

If music were to be regarded as singing in general, whether professionally or unprofessionally, CPc is extensively used. This is because CPc's songs are sung almost everywhere in Cameroon. This includes churches, schools and ceremonies of different sorts. I am considering music here from a very professional perspective. Many scholars mentioned that musicians use CPc in music (Schröder, 2003; Fonka, 2014c). However, Mbangwana (2004) refers to Lapiro de Mbanga's music, which has brought in a new style of pidgin common to youths. Mbangwana (ibid.) is concerned with the different varieties of CPc and not with music. He seems to be one of the few scholars who have gone beyond just describing the use of pidgin by musicians. He has analysed the language variety used by Lapiro. Table 6.1 presents the innovative use of pidgin assembled from different songs of Lapiro de Mbanga by Mbangwana (2004, p. 31).

Table 6.1 Creations in Pidgin

Innovative creations in Pidgin	English equivalence
Buka	to play card
njamanjama	Vegetables
nyama	to eat
tum	to sell
yang	to buy
chaka	Shoes
ndiba	Water
tut	to carry
dangwa	Dance
nga	Girlfriend
jobajo	Beaufort
kwikkwik	Quickly
nayo nayo	Slowly

This kind of usage as is the case with Camfranglais or slanguage as Mbangwana (2006, p. 220) calls it "induces friendliness or intimacy in a very profound way" among its speakers.

Ubanako (2015) asserts that the use of Pidgin English in music by Anglophones and Francophone Cameroonians has been very high. In listing the domain in which CPc is used in Cameroon, Ubanako (ibid.) says the domains of ethnic or cultural manifestations in CPE include music. This section, therefore, affirms the presence of CPc in music.

THEORETICAL CONSIDERATION

This work is examined under the Social Conflict Theory propagated by Karl Marx. The conflict theory claims that society is in perpetual conflict because of competition for limited resources. It holds that social order is maintained by domination and power rather than consensus and conformity. According to conflict theory, those with wealth and power try to hold on to it by any means possible, chiefly by suppressing the poor and powerless. This theory argues that individuals and groups (social classes) have differing amounts of material and non-material resources (such as the wealthy vs. the poor) and that the more powerful groups use their power to exploit groups with less power. Thus, the social conflict theory states that groups within a capitalist society tend to interact in a destructive way that allows no mutual benefit and little cooperation. According to Karl Marx, two major social groups exist in all stratified societies: a ruling class and a subject class. The ruling class derives its power from its ownership and control of the forces of production. The ruling class exploits and oppresses the subject class. As a result, the two classes have a fundamental conflict of interest.

This theory holds that social order is maintained by domination and power rather than consensus and conformity. Sears (2008) strengthens this theory when he emphasises that societies are defined by inequality that produces conflict rather than that which produces order and consensus. Based on inequality, this conflict can only be overcome through a fundamental transformation of the existing relations in society and is productive of new social relations. Human potential (e.g., capacity for creativity) is suppressed by conditions of exploitation and oppression, which are necessary in any society with an unequal division of labour. The uneven distribution within the conflict theory was predicted to be maintained through ideological coercion, where the bourgeoisie would force acceptance of the current conditions by the proletariat. Marx further believed that as the working class and poor were subjected to worsening conditions, a collective consciousness would bring the inequality to light and potentially result in revolt. If conditions were subsequently adjusted to address the concerns of the proletariat, the conflict circle would eventually repeat.

Based on this background, Lapiro de Mbanga, who can be termed the mouthpiece of the oppressed, has sung his songs. The language used in his songs does not end at condemning systems; it attacks individuals, thus creating conflict that does not necessarily solve the problem he is out to decry. Otomar and Wehr (2002) think that as the new millennium begins, conflict actors must learn not only how to deescalate destructive conflicts but also how to utilise "constructive" conflicts: how to clarify their own goals, how to select conflict strategies and tactics rationally; and how to apply them to achieve their goals while minimising the costs. The language used by this author seems not to consider the fact that in achieving his goals, he has to minimise the cost. Lapiro de Mbanga has on several occasions been arrested and locked up not only because he exposes political ills and injustice meted on the people by leaders but because he attacks those who have been responsible for such oppressions. This is a costly thing many musicians would minimise or avoid by using general statements. Though this might be out of fear of the political leaders, it is cost-effective because it is a living person who can hope to see change happen, not a dead one.

It will not be wrong to think that it is from such a background that Cloke (2001, p. 210-211) asserts the following:

> Power stimulates a strong set of emotions and actions on both sides, particularly when it takes the form of power over others, rather than over us. For those who possess it, there is arrogance, abusiveness, corruption, fear, and guilt. Those who seek to wrest it from others experience an equally powerful set of effects, including jealousy, impotence, rage, ambition, fear, amorality, greed, internal splits, blaming, brutalisation, demonisation, and revenge. Power is easier by far to condemn than to exercise fairly, causing many to prefer the safety of cynicism and making it dangerous to translate criticism of what is wrong into concrete proposals for systemic change.

This is the type of environment in which Lapiro de Mbanga sings, a chaotic and repressive environment.

METHODOLOGY

The data used in this paper are collected from the songs of a renowned musician who uses pidgin in his songs not only to send out his messages but also to deploy bitter and hurting expressions which are either consciously or unconsciously meant to hurt, thus engendering conflict. This musician, who is considered by Cameroonians, especially young people attracted to his songs as the father of the Mboko pidgin, is Lapiro de Mbanga. Two of his songs, "démissioner" and "lefam so," are presented and analysed. These songs are sung in CPc and per the definition of insults and spear words, I judge them to be littered with insults and spear words. Of the two songs, "démissioner" has been transcribed, while for "lefam so," only concerned excerpts have been employed.

PRESENTATION AND ANALYSIS OF DATA

As I indicated in the methodology, the song transcribed is "démissioner" (resign) by Lapiro de Mbanga. This song is presented below before an analysis of excerpts is done later. The presentation of the whole song is because the pidgin used is an uncommonly spoken variety among Cameroonians and also because the words chosen for analyses will make sense if examined within the context of use. Given the language's technicality and length, I have not translated the song into English. However, I have translated all the excerpts used for analysis. The second song has not been transcribed in its entirety. Only some portions have been transcribed, and analysable excerpts are extracted.

Démissioner

Démissioner (5x)
Ou fall ngombe yu meik laik sei yu noba hier.

   Fo insaid lachete yu giv dat coup de tête wei yu donc teik sisha Erik Chinje bikos yu bin get ma makabo sins yia ba yia an a hau donc go bata moi yu nie fo dat affair fo constitution. Fo constitution, yu profit fo emeurt fo fevrier 2008, yu send Tabi fo baksaid, i go bolo njoh ngata fo tri yie... donc yu tu sabi sei popo yu donc fan am, yu don trouvam an yu mos supot am. Fo supot am, yu mos tai hat yu chop metris bikos conformament a l'article 19 fo...international fo nations unis, an according to motion de soutien an appelle du people wei ma complice dem don giv mi, a go spit faya jos nau laik dragon pwaa. Na tsounami a de declancher fo dis heur. I get folere fo ai. I no de giv kong, i don dame' rash bikos popo mi a sabi sei dis tour, no bi ngata egen, na fo teme mi en direct an mi a dei pres fo meng. De tous les façon, a bi don preter sermant from fo yia bai yia sei a go domo, donc.

   A sei uwo, dat equip fo lions indomitable wei yu don noie fo besier fo Kondenguie an besier fo Newbel dei so wei na popo yu don formé yi. Yes, na yu... equip national de shiba, na yu sep sep don recruite jouer an na yu meik dem licence; na yu bi selectioneur, coach an captain jouer ; na yu de meik classement fo ndamba ; na yu bi preparateur physique, soigneur an na yu bi....Trente ans de championa, yu don compose trente quartre equipe. Wuna don buka ndamba fo ol kan kan stat dem... sep so, soso defect bikos of ova bombom. Kodri man, ndamba no bi bombom; ndamba na sens.

   Step daun, demissioner bikos yu don ova massacre constitution. Fo reglement interieur fo yu democracie avancé a grande vitesse, pouvoir executive, pouvoir judiciel an pouvoir legislative na yu de piloter. Sote yu don teik president fo Assemblé National yu meik garçon de pus wei yu de commissioner yi fo go representer yu fo mbout evenement fo lasa pays dem. Yu don ova echouer, ... Yu don teik justice meik kwara fo bole dans les siasia pipo wei dei de gener yu njoh. Insecurite generaliser, ... yu don ova mouille ... privatisation des produits toxiques fo societes...

wei de giv pipo cancer. Insecurité généralisé, ... *demande massacré ya represantant, chef de terre monsieur le sous prefet ana kamaboro fo Bakassi. Yu don ova mouillé....*

Sapeur pompier don ton snek sote na dem de saf ndiba, yes na faya brigad de saf ston fo zhong fo ngola an na minista fo santé de komnie fo da kolo hau wei dem de savam pipo. Yi de wait taim weih dem go santeé fo kondenguier bifo he publier yi oun lettre fo bra sei « Javais dit que. J'avais fait que. Je voulais même demissioné » so na so... Fo sika ova ngeme ana chômage wei yu don multiplié fo dis mboko, bensikineurs, chauffeurs clando, laveurs des voitures, takleur, sauveteur, bai am selam, coiffeuses ana coiffeurs ambullant for marché central, kol boks, ingenier for nchounko de pointé fo don ren an fo don son...

No bi dem di kilibili bébé fo matarnité fo sai ba sai. No bi yua bolo na securisation des personnes et leurs biens, a vrais dire, da wan na echouason total if yu no fit guaranti sucurité sep fo nourrisons... Yu don electrocuté code electoral, terminateur de terminator. Yu parti no get long fo siege de restitution for ngola, yi de skwaté fo palais de congrés. No bi na shem dis.express de skwaté la... don no bi daso faut fo jouer. Popo yu sep no dei wel. Yu lep brasa yu step daun. Ta bi sei yu mos demissioné laik yu répé, grand camarade wei bi dash yu chia an wei yu don abandoné fo Dakar. Popo yu pa Paul dem don vote yu na sei meik yu gerer.

Yu don nomé ya jouer sei meik dem gérer. *Normalement for gerer dem mos touché. If yu toucher yu mos taché. But au lieu que yu toucher daso yu don bata go taché. Da bin sei yu don put ndoti.... Papa yu mos signé mandat, yu mos bote yie yie ; yu mos joua da ngata, yu mos bolo cuvé moto yu mos signé mandat.*

Besides the above transcription, I also present instances where the same author used insults and spear words in another song. These will be indicated in the analysis. I will begin by examining insults on individuals by the artist as seen in the transcribed song.

Insults and spear words in Lapiro's music

It should be noted that these insults and spear words enveloped in CPc are directed mainly at the president of Cameroon, Paul Biya and his government. Lapiro is very direct in his attack on both the regime and the head of state. I have classified them under two main headings: institutional attack and personal attack. He uses conflict generation language to decry the poor management of public resources.

Conflict generation language

The following statements from the transcribed song are considered conflict generation language, not only because they criticise the regime but also because they create two camps: the ruling class, which bears the insults, and the oppressed class. The following excerpts represent language that generates conflict from "démissioner."

1. Wuna don buka ndamba fo ol kan kan stat dem… sep so, soso defait bikos of ova
   You have played ball in all kinds of stadia…even so, always losing because of bombom. Kodri man, ndamba no bi bombom; ndamba na sens.
   Senselessness. My friend, football is not senselessness; football is tact.
2. yu don ova massacre constitution.
   You have over-meddled with the constitution.
3. Yu don ova echouer…
   You have over-failed
4. Yu don teik justice meik kwara fo bole dans les iasia people wei dei de gener yu njoh.
   You have used justice as a hidden means to freely terminate those who trouble you.
5. yu don ova mouille … (2x)
   you have over failed.
6. Fo sika ova ngeme ana chômage wei yu don multiplié fo dis mboko
   Because of entrenched poverty and unemployment that you have increased in this country.
7. No bi ya bolo na securisation des personnes et leurs biens ? A vrais dire, da wan
   Is your job not to provide security to persons and property? Frankly speaking, that
   na echouason total if yu no fit guaranti sucurité sep fo nourrisons…
   is total failure if you cannot guarantee even the safety of babies.
8. Popo yu sep no dey wel.
   Paul you are not well yourself
9. Mola puis que généralement dan vampire dem no de bolo (*From Lefam so Lefam so*)

Friend, whereas those vampires generally do not work

From the data presented from excerpt (1) to (7), there are many common grammatical elements that can generate conflict. The personal pronoun "wuna" ("you" in the second person plural), "yu' ("you" in the second person singular), "dem" ("they") are statements of blame and dissatisfaction. In (1), (2) and (3) above, the statements which accuse the president and his leadership team as incompetent would obviously create conflict because the accusation can only be true for those who are on Lapiro de Mbanga's side, but not for those on the side of the president. People may choose not to see what convincingly the reality before them is, or they may decide to see from another perspective. Furlong (2005, pp. 31-33) calls this problem of data differential - one party has data that the other doesn't have. I would rather say, one party decides to view data differently from the other even if there is the possibility of seeing it the same way. He presents data points to support this conflict situation wherein different people see the same thing differently. Figure 6.1 below presents a situation using data points.

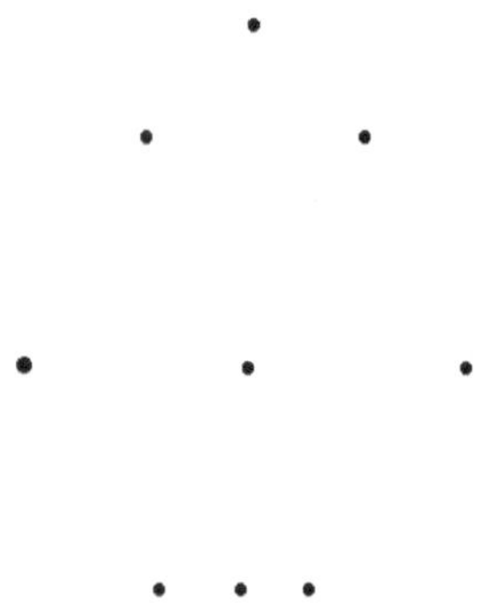

Figure 6.1 Data points

From this data point differential view, it is possible to create conflict in anything we say, especially when such is opened to debate. The data points in Figure 6.1 are viewed differently by two different people in Figures 6.2 and 6.3. It can get further complicated if the third person decides to see in yet another picture. This, however, does not cancel the possibility that the two can view it in the same manner to avoid conflict. The words 'wuna,' 'dem,' and 'yu' draw a line between the person insulting and the person(s) being insulted. The social conflict theory is evident here because one group (the ruling class) is considered oppressing the masses (represented by the musician).

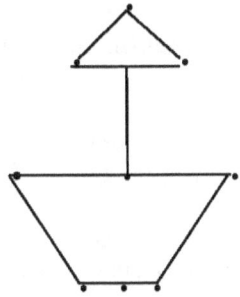

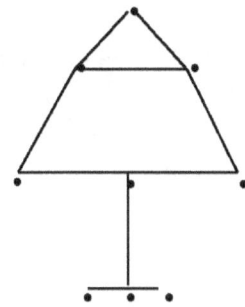

Figure 6.2 Data point differential view

Figure 6.3 Same data point differential view from another angle

Conflict Generation Language on institution

1. Yu parti no get long fo siege de restitution for ngola, I de skwaté fo palais de congrés.
   (Your party has no headquarters in Cameroon, they are patching up at the congress hall).
2. No bi na sheim dis?
   (Is this not a shame?)

In (10), Lapiro attacks a political party, the Cameroon People's Democratic Party (CPDM). This is taking conflict from an individual to a large scale, thereby multiplying the number of enemies because a political party is an institution and an attack on it provokes anger from different angles. This is an insult that induces pain. This particular insult has nothing to do about the wellbeing of the population; rather, it can be said that Lapiro is frustrated to the point that anything related to the person in power should be condemned. Lapiro understands that he is piercing and the result could be death, "mi a sabi sei dis tour, no bi ngata egen, na fo teme mi en direct an mi a dei pres fo meng *(I know that this time it won't be imprisonment again, it will be to kill me at once and I am ready to die).* Even if this bravery pleases his supporters, who are giving him "motion de soutien" *(motion of support)*, it exposes him to counter attacks. CPc cannot, in this circumstance of exposure, provide any form of shield to the singer. The CPDM party also has young people who understand this youthful language and they will not hesitate to interpret the insults to the party's hierarchy for necessary action. Language only becomes as shield in the case where nobody is interested in listening to what that language carries.

Conflict generation Language on individuals

The following are examples of language use that target the individual directly:
    a.   yu sen Tabi fo baksaid
        (you sent Tabi behind the house (Killed))
    b.   Step daun
        (resign)
    c.   …demande massacré ya represant, chef de terre monsieur le sous prefet …Bakassi
        (orders the killing of your representative, the sub-prefect…Bakassi)
    d.   Yu don electrocuté code electoral…
        (you have short circuited the electoral code)
    e.   Yu lep brasa yu step daun.
        (abandon captainship and step down)
    f.   Da bi sei yu mos demissioné laik yu répé, grand camarade wei bin dash yu chiar an
        (this means you must resign like your father, the great comrade, who offered you the sit
        wei yu don abandoné fo Dakar
        and whom you have abandoned in Dakar)
    g.   Papa, yu mos signé mandate
        (father you must sign a warrant)
    h.   yu mos joua da ngata,
        (you must go to prison)
    i.   yu mos bolo cuvé moto
        (you must do hard labour)

More of conflict creation is seen in this section with spear words directed at the president in the following ways:

Accusation for murder – in (a) and (c) above, the president is accused of having orchestrated the murder of some personalities. Vote of no confidence – in (b), I, and (f) he orders the president to resign. The use of "mos" (must) signals disrespect because Lapiro speaks as if he is from the ruling class whereas he is from the repressed. Sentences – (g), (h) and (i), he says what most African leaders will not want to hear. This sentence indicates that whenever he steps down, whether willingly or by force, he will have to pay for the crimes he has been accused of.

The cost of such charges, especially from a very disadvantaged position, is always very high, given that according to Marx's theory of social conflict, social order is maintained by domination and power, rather than consensus and conformity. When a collective consciousness brings the inequality to light and potentially results in revolt, the ruling class can be removed from power. It is dangerous for an individual without a collective backing to fight a regime. Fighting as an individual invites easy repressive measures from the authorities, but fighting as a group makes any repressive measure difficult.

WHY THE USE OF MBOKO VARIETY OF CPC?

The musician, whose works are of interest to this paper, deploys not just pidgin but a brand common to some group of youths for a number of reasons. The question this section seeks to answer is whether or not the variety of pidgin used by this musician can serve as a shield. In other words, can the message passed across in this variety make understanding difficult for some Cameroonians? I will attempt to answer this question by bringing out the characteristics of the Mboko variety and whether or not these characteristics can render the variety discrete.

CHARACTERISTICS OF MBOKO VARIETY

What makes a variety of language distinct from the other is its characteristics. Varieties of CPc are considered distinct from each other based on phraseological differences, unfamiliar lexical usage (the case of Mboko variety), difference in accents and many others. The following are considered the characteristics of the Mboko variety of CPc: Unfamiliar lexical application, multiple language merging and voluntary lexical adaptation.

Unfamiliar lexical application

Unfamiliar lexical application seems to be the most renowned feature of the Mboko variety of CPc. This has to do with the use of lexical items which are the creation of the speaker and not borrowed items from any exiting language. The audience are obliged to learn such new lexical items and their meanings. It is in these items that the speaker somewhat hides the meaning of what he wants to say. Examples of such items employed in the songs chosen for this study are:

Table 6.2 Unfamiliar Lexical items

words	Meanings
sisha	Threaten
bolo	Work
ngata	Prison
damer	To eat or food
meng	Die
domo	Fight
kilibili	Kidnap
buka	Play
Njaka	Children
boler	Finish
nier	See

Though some of these words may seem so familiar to Cameroonians, especially CPc speakers, it is a creation of a specific group of people, which is employed in music generally to hide meaning because the speakers of this variety also speak the normal pidgin when they are conversing with other people.

Multiple language merging

It can be argued that multiple language merging is not a characteristic specific to the Mboko variety of CPc because there is no language that does not employ borrowing from other languages found in the same environment. This merging is different from Camfranglais that uses the same languages, English, French, local language and even this variety of CPc in that, Camfranglais simply brings the items together and use them as a new language, while Mboko speakers reform the words borrowed from other languages to sound different and look new.

Example
1. Yu mos joua da ngata (*you must be imprisoned*)
   (*you must enjoy that prison*)
2. I don damer rash (*I am angry*)
   I have eaten anger
3. Mola puis que generallement, dan vampire dem no de bolo (*friend, those vampires generally do not work*)
   (*Mola whereas generally, those vampires do not work*)

These sentences are a combination of English, French and the lexical creations such as ngata (prison), damer (eat) and bolo (work), which make this variety distinct and beautiful. These lexical creations are not from any known language; the lexemes that make this variety stand out.

Voluntary lexical adaptation

Lexical adaptation is borrowing, which is defined as the process by which a word from one language is adapted for use in another. The dominant language may assume the role of lexical donor, providing certain kinds of words or morphemes to be selected by speakers of the recessive language for adoption while the recessive language system becomes the recipient of the "donated" words and morphemes, acting as a kind of morphosyntactic matrix into which these elements are grafted (Thomason and Kaufman, 1988, p. 48; Thomason, 2001, p. 85–91) cited in Field (2002, p. 2). It can be argued that French and English words in Mboko variety cannot be considered borrowing because that is what the language is made of. This paper, however, considers some voluntary lexical adaptation whereby unlike the normal borrowing, words taken from the French language by Lapiro de Mbanga are not as a result of any deficit in the recessive language and are not used in the original form. They are given a new form to make them neither French nor English, but Mboko variety. Some of these words are seen on Table 6.3.

Table 6.3 lexical adaptation

Words and example	Word in the donor language	Meaning in English
Kasha- katika fo Ngola an yi chinda dem don kasha… (*the boss and his followers in Yaounde have …*)	Cashier- Noun (English) and caissier- noun (French)	A person who handles the cash register at various locations. (used here as a verb- to collect)
Trouvam- you donc fin am, yu don trouvam (*you have searched and you have found*)	Trouver- verb (French)	Trouv- am is French lexeme 'trouve' (found) and a pidgin particle **'am'** (it)
Echouason- da wan na echouason total (*that is total failure*)	Echouer- verb (French)	Failure in French is 'echec' not 'echouason'
Skwater- yi de skwater fo palais de congrés (*it is squatting in the congress hall*)	Squat- verb (English)	Occupy a place illegally. (Does not exist in French in the same form)

From Table 6.3 above, the words taken from either French or English used in Mboko variety of pidgin are different from the way they are understood in their original context. 'trouv am' for example, adopted from the French word "trouver" (to find) but used as a pidgin word by adding the 'am' (it) pronoun that comes after most pidgin verbs.

The discreetness of some Mboko variety

Not all varieties of a language spoken in a speech community are understood by everybody in that community. Although the people may share the same norms, some varieties are created for specific purposes by members within a speech community to inhibit others from having access to their information. The pidgin used here, especially in Lapiro de Mbanga's songs, is not a popular pidgin which is opened to understanding by every pidgin-speaking Cameroonian. He uses the variety of Cameroon Pidgincreole that is popular only to a particular kind of people. Though a youthful variety, not all youths understand it. The term "youth" is a flexible and contestable social category that can be variously reproduced in different social and cultural contexts (Leppänen, 2007, p. 151). The youth variety of CPc is otherwise called Mboko variety (Fonka, 2011; 2014a), a variety which estranges itself from the pidgin that most youths, children and elders speak, a variety associated more to park boys. Mboko variety to a certain extend is a restrained variety, but not completely out of reach as whoever wants to understand what is said can go ahead and enquire.

The use of Mboko variety in particular is meant to amuse and draw support from those who understand it. The youthful group that speaks this variety are mainly school dropouts who are engaged in activities which necessitate more input and less benefit. The language of such people is always rebellious, thus they will support its use. This goes to support the following statement Lapiro de Mbanga makes at the beginning of the song *demissioner* - "*an according to motion de soutien an appelle du people wei ma complice dem don giv mi, a go spit faya jos nau laik dragon pwaa.*" (*And following the motions of support and the people's call that my friends have given me, I will spit fire now like a dragon*). This is an indication that this is a language with speakers and Lapiro de Mbanga, the father of this variety recognises his followers. People cannot just follow him without understanding the message he is sending out. They know that he is using his songs to fight a common enemy.

RECOMMENDATIONS

The following recommendations can be helpful to avoid deadly confrontations when clamouring for a change in society.

a. It is quite true that there exist codes that groups use to attempt to shield information from filtering out to other groups with different ideologies. No language is completely discrete because every language can be learned and spoken by whosoever wants to speak it. Some members of the in-group can interpret hidden codes to members of the out-group. This means the Mboko variety of CPc can be a battle shield only as long as the information it carries does not call for public attention. Avoid creating conflict using a particular language by thinking that it will not be understood.
b. Following the theory used in this study, social change comes when a people collectively revolt against a repressive regime and unseat it. If it has been deadly for leaders with a great following like Martin Luther King Jr, to cause change, it will not be better with an individual who could be brandished as rebelling against legitimate regimes. Conflict should be constructive to the individual and the community, not destructive as it is the case with most conflicts around the world. Uline et al. (2003), holds that conflict, when well-managed, breathes life and energy into relationships and can cause individuals to be much more innovative and productive. Individuals should not engage in fighting regimes, group mobilisation is advisable.
c. When there are national events, musicians come together and compose one song which reflects their unity in diversity. A concerned musician who cares about the wellbeing of citizens should mobilise a college of musicians to stand up as one person against repression in a single album. It is easy, in this case, to get the masses aligned behind them and cause national consciousness. It will also be difficult for a repressive regime to launch a crackdown in such a case.

CONCLUSION

This chapter set out to show how Lapiro de Mbanga through music uses a variety of CPc, Mboko variety, as a shield to hide himself against attack and also as a weapon to attack a corrupt and repressive regime. CPc is considered to play a dual function here, a battle weapon and a battle shield. After presenting and analysing the data for this study, it brings out some of the lexemes that make the variety considered difficult to understand by out-group members. A very intelligent adaptation of English and French, and French and pidgin combinations giving birth to words like in "trouv- am," make this variety also interesting to listen to.

Although Lapiro uses the Mboko variety of CPc to attack the authorities, the goal is probably to provide a provocative stimulus, with the hope of moving them to think more deeply and, ultimately, to act more prudently. The aim is to moralise the people addressed, in the words of Uline et al. (2003, p. 782), "cause the individual to be much more innovative and productive." It might also have been to draw the attention of the repressed to revolt and overpower the ruling class. Whichever it was, the words are sharp, direct and provocative. Although they are good enough to create awareness, they are also bad enough to bring harm to the musician who stands to speak as an individual, and to his fans and faithful listeners, who are prone to attacks and arrest from a repressive government. This paper holds that language is only discrete as long as the audience is not interested in the information it carries.

REFERENCES

Alobwede, D. C. (1998). Banning Pidgin English in Cameroon? *English Today 53* 14 (1), 54-60.

Atechi, S. (2011). Is Cameroon Pidgin flourishing or dying? *English Today*. 27(3), 30-34.

Atechi, S. & Fonka, H. (2007). *Pidgin English as a Lingua Franca in Cameroon*. In Papers in English & Linguistics (PEL), 7&8, 40-55.

Ayafor, M. (2005). Kamtok (Pidgin) is Gaining Ground in Cameroon. In E. Chia (Ed.). *African Linguistics and the Development of African Communities* (pp. 191-199). CODESRIA.

Chia, E. (2009). Further developments in Cameroon Pidgin English. In *Annals of the Faculty of Arts Letters and Social Sciences*. Festschrift in Honour of Professor Paul Mbangwana. Les Grandes Editions, 39-50.

Cloke, K. (2001). *Mediating dangerously: the frontiers of conflict resolution*. John Wiley & Sons.

Field, W. F. (2002). *Linguistic borrowing in bilingual contexts*. John Benjamins Publishing.

Fonka, H. (2022). Cameroon Pidgincreole English as a Fire Extinguisher: The Case of the Anglophone Crisis. In A. Ngefac (Ed.). *Aspects of Cameroon Englishes*, (pp. 130-147). Cambridge Scholars Publishing.

Fonka, H. (2019). Is Cameroon Pidgin English a Pidgin, a Pidgincreole or a creole? In T. Mbuh and E. Samba. *Bordered Identities in Language, Literature and Culture: Reading in Cameroon and the Global Space*. (pp. 97-112). Cambridge Scholars

Publishing.

Fonka, H. (2014b). Can Cameroon Pidgincreole for Cameroon Schools Improve Education and Nation Building? In E. Veyu and V. Ubanako (Eds.). *Faultlines in Postcoloniality: Contemporary Readings*. (pp. 148-168). Cambridge Scholars Publishing.

Fonka, H. (2014a). Cameroon Pidgincreole (CPc): Focus on New Linguistic and Cultural Borders. In V. Ubanako and J. Anderson (Eds.). *Crossing Linguistic Borders in Postcolonial Anglophone Africa* (pp. 69- 86). Cambridge Scholars Publishing.

Fonka, H. (2011). Cameroon Pidgin English: Evolution in Attitudes, Functions and Varieties. An unpublished PhD Thesis. University of Yaounde I.

Furlong, G. T. (2005). *The conflict resolution toolbox: models & maps for analyzing, diagnosing, and resolving conflict*. John Wiley & Sons Canada.

Kouega, J. P. (2001). Pidgin English Facing Death in Cameroon. *Terralingua*: Hancock. 11-22.

Leppänen, S. (2007). Youth Language in Media Context: insights into the Functions of Language in Finland. In *World Englishes*, 26 (2), 149-169.

Mbangwana, P. (2006). Some Aspects of Home-grown Speech of Francophone Students: The case of Clipping and Blend. In P. Mbangwana, K. Mpoche and T. Mbuh, (Eds.). *Language Literature and Identity*. (pp. 220- 226). Culillier Verlag.

Mbangwana, P. (2004). Pidgin English in Cameroon: a veritable linguistic Menu. In Echu George and Obeng, S. G. eds, Africa *Meets Europe: Language in West Africa*. Nova Science Publishers. 23-44.

Mbangwana, P. (1983). The Scope and Role of Pidgin English in Cameroon. In K. Edna, E. Chia and J. Povey (Eds.). *The Sociolinguistic Profile of Urban Centres in Cameroon*. (pp. 79-92). Crossroads Press.

MTD Training (2010). Dealing with Conflict and Complaints. Ventus Publishing. http://promeng.eu/downloads/training-materials/ebooks/soft-skills/dealing-with-conflict-

Neba, A., Fogwe E., & Atindogb, G. (2006). "Cameroon Pidgin English (CPE) as a Tool for Empowerment and National Development". In *African Study Monograph*. Kurenai: Textversion. 27(2), 39-61.

Neu, J. (2008). *Sticks and Stones: The Philosophy of Insults*. Oxford University Press.

Ngefach, A. & Sala B. (2006). Cameroon Pidgin and Cameroon English at a Confluence. In *English World Wide*. Amsterdam: John Benjamins. 27, 217-227.

Otomar, B. and Wehr, P. (2002). *Using Conflict Theory*. Cambridge University Press,

Robert, B. C. (1991). *Random House Webster's College*. Random House of Canada.

Sala, B. (2009). Writing in Cameroon Pidgin English: begging the question. In *English Today* 98 25(2), 11-17.

Sala, B. (2006). Does Cameroonian English have grammatical norms? In *English Today* 88, 22 (4) 59-64.

Schröder, A. (2003). *Status, Functions and Prospects of Pidgin English*. Grunter Narr Verlag Tübingen.

Sears, A. (2008). *A Good Book in Theory: A Guide to Theoretical Thinking. Higher Education University*. University of Toronto Press.

Simo-Bobda, A. (2009). Keynote Paper". In *Annals of the Faculty of Arts Letters and Social Sciences*. Festschrift in Honour of Professor Paul Mbangwana. Les Grandes Editions,17-26.

Simo-Bobda, A. (2001). Verifying Statuses and Perceptions of English in Cameroon: A Diachronic and Synchronic Analysis. In TRANS. Internet Zeitschrift für Kulturwissenchaften. N° 11. www.http://www.inst.at/trans/11Nr/bobda 11.htm.

Ubanako, V. (2015). Cameroon Pidgin English at the Service of Local Culture, Science and Technology. In International Journal of Language and Linguistics. 3(6), 510-515.

Uline, C. L, Tschannen-Moran, M. & Perez, L. (2003). Constructive Conflict: How Controversy Can Contribute to School Improvement. *Teachers College Record*. 105 (5), 782–816.

7

Mitigating Linguistic Identity Differences in Cameroon
The Role of Bilingual Education

KIWOH TERENCE NSAI

Language is a central feature of human identity. When someone is heard speaking, guesses can be made on several things about him or her. Beyond this, language is a powerful symbol of national and ethnic identity (Spolsky, 1999). The use of a particular language leads to some identification of the individual. However, there are possibilities of someone speaking a specific language but not belonging to the community where such a language is used. This truism makes Bucholtz (1999) affirm that such an individual who embraces a particular language, which is not his/hers, engages in a positive identity practice. Therefore, the language that anyone speaks becomes an important but not the only instrument of identification. Anzaldua (1987, p. 59) corroborates this by saying there is only a thin line between language and identity. She adds that "Ethnic [national] identity is twin skin to linguistic identity – I am my language." In multilingual and bilingual communities, authorities have often had to handle issues related to language and identity, as citizens tend to develop loyalties and identities towards particular language groups.

However, new linguistic identities have been constructed using education. Adger (1998), Bucholtz (1999), and Fordham (1998) have specifically studied the construction of new identities for further integration among Spanish-English-speaking students in the United States of America. Models and aims of such constructions are illustrated in Baker (1999). In Cameroon, studies on language and identity have been carried out. Among such studies are Mpoche (2006), Chiatoh (2006) and Biloa (2012). They dwell on problems that the co-existence of Francophones and Anglophones has created. But, studies on the construction of a new official language identity are difficult to come by.

This chapter posits that Cameroon could have a new official language identity through bilingual education. Such an identity can go a long way to solve some of the problems identified by Biloa, Mpoche and Chiatoh. Before proceeding to show how this new identity can be constructed, it is essential to examine what is meant here by bilingual education.

Hamers and Blanc (1989) give a peculiar definition of bilingual education. Their simple definition is that bilingual education is a system that allows instruction in two languages at a particular moment. For any educational system to be viewed as bilingual, the learning process should be in two languages and occur within a particular period. This excludes curricula where a second or foreign language is taught as a subject within a school system, with no other use in other learning-related activities. Ovando (2003) identifies two main types of bilingual education. These are the transitional and maintenance types. The transitional type is found in a situation where learners of a second language are being prepared to integrate a second language community. In such a case, they use their first and second languages to learn. The maintenance type is adopted to keep certain linguistic traditions and cultures alive. Spolsky (2009) reports a typical case in Israel where the State adopts a bilingual education programme to maintain Hebrew.

Bilingual education has many objectives. Baker (1999, p. 151) lists ten objectives ranging from assimilation of individuals into a mainstream culture, unifying a multi-ethnic community, and preserving ethnic and religious identities to deepening the understanding of languages and cultures. Each nation that adopts a bilingual education programme has one of these objectives that it intends to attain. Cameroon adopted a bilingual culture with two official languages to unite the two dominant colonial cultures, English and French, which co-exist in the polity. However, a carefully designed bilingual education programme for Cameroon can further consolidate national unity, strengthen nationhood, and create a new identity for the people. Thus, this paper is based on the assertion that a carefully planned early bilingual education programme can contribute to developing a new official language identity in Cameroon.

Data used to corroborate arguments raised here is collected through interviews, observations and recording authorities' day-to-day comments and declarations. In addition, scientific and newspaper articles related to the question under study are vibrant data sources here. Finally, school programmes of existing bilingual education structures are also consulted. Statistical data were obtained from several institutions. These are HOBEC Bonaberi-Douala, New Century Bilingual Academy Mfandena – Yaoundé, COSBIE Mendong-Yaoundé and *Sainte Brigitte* Up station, Bamenda. The data were analysed and presented using simple percentages. The analysis will examine the state of national unity in Cameroon, which justifies our call for a new official language identity.

THE STATE OF NATIONAL UNITY IN CAMEROON

According to the Constitution of 18 January 1996, Cameroon has two official languages with equal status. These exist under an official bilingualism policy in which French and English are used. This linguistic marriage came as a result of the reunification in 1961 of former West (British) Cameroon(s) and the former French Cameroon (*La République du Cameroun*). The nation's official appellation has since evolved from a Federal Republic after the plebiscite of 1961 to a United Republic after the 1972 referendum and to a Republic through a Presidential Decree in 1984. As demonstrated below, citizens from both sides of the linguistic divide hold very much to the cultures they inherited from the colonial powers (Biloa & Echu, 2008). Both languages, co-existing in a highly politically and administratively centralised republic, have given birth to identity crises. These crises reached their peaks in the 1990s, with the Anglophones holding what came to be known as the All Anglophone Conference (AAC I and II) in Buea (2nd to 3rd April 1993) and Bamenda (1st May 1994), respectively. During these conferences, the Anglophones called for a stop to their marginalisation in Cameroon. According to Anchimbe (2005, p. 12), this marginalisation is manifested by the fact that: "In the late 1990s and even today, administration (in Cameroon) is conceived in French and only translated (if need be) into English. The military, the National Assembly, treaties, and diplomatic exchanges are arraigned in French." Bilingualism which is supposed to be a distinguishing feature of the Republic, according to Jikong (2003, p. 4), has been reduced to a mere slogan. He strongly asserts this in the following terms:

> One of the major reasons accounting for the assertion that state bilingualism is a mere slogan resides in the way in which high level appointments are made in the civil service. It is not a secret that monolingual civil servants, presidents, ministers etc … still litter our landscape in their majority (…) that is why a completely English illiterate Divisional Officer can serve in Su-Bum without any qualms.

Whereas it is a pre-requisite for any top civil servant in the Cameroon administration of Anglophone origin to speak French, nothing obliges his French-speaking counterpart to speak English. Incidents like that in the Oku

Sub-Division of Bui Division where a divisional officer addressed a group of the local population in French, ignoring calls to order from his immediate hierarchy, the senior divisional officer have been documented. He was addressing a group of peasant farmers who needed help to understand their first official language, English, and talk less of understanding French, their second official language.[1] During the politically hot years (1989-1994), many English-speaking Cameroonians claimed to have suffered some form of injustice just because of their first official language, English. This group allegedly received names that linked them to political opponents of the regime in power (Mpoche, 2006, Nsahlai, nd).

In daily interaction, the two linguistic groups have shown much hostility to each other. It is common to hear words like *frog, francofool* and *francobête*. These words, coming from Anglophone Cameroonians, describe their French-speaking fellow citizens. The same goes for the Anglophones who are described by their French-speaking countrymen as *Bamenda* (meaning an idiot and docile in behaviour and someone who could be easily manipulated), *les anglos, les gauchies, les opposants* etc. In fact, Anglophones and Francophones in Cameroon look at each other highly suspiciously. When it comes to choices in marriage, very few parents readily give the go-ahead for their children to get married to persons of the other linguistic group.[2] The malaise culminated in a major civil strife in 2016, with a rebellion that has lasted to October 2023, in what can be described as the second phase of the Anglophone crisis.

Concerning education at the level of secondary schools, some students still consider the time allocated for French and English languages as time to rest or go home. As some French-speaking students put it, *"C'est Dieu qui donne l'anglais* or *Dieudonné,"* translating the fact that a pass in English is almost a mystery. At the beginning of the 2012/2013 academic year, the Ministry of Secondary Education introduced a new programme in which some standard arts and science subjects were suppressed in the English sub-system of education.[3] The Anglophone educational community viewed this as an attempt to

---

1 This information was relayed by *The Herald Newspaper* of 16th August 1991, p. 3
2 Kiwoh (upcoming) "Marriage across official language frontiers: A factor of National Integration in Cameroon?"
3 This information was relayed by the Cameroon Teachers Trade Union (CATTU) in the CRTV Radio Sunday morning programme Cameroon Calling of September 23, 2012. The Executive Secretary of CATTU was calling on all educational stakeholders of the English sub-system to stand up against what he described as "attempts to wipe out" the Anglophone system of education by educational authorities. It is alleged that after some negotiations, the new programme was suspended.

wipe out their educational system and a sign of bad faith from Francophone educational authorities who have shown their inability to apply resolutions of the 1995 Education Forum held in Kribi.

In the university milieu, Anglophones consistently complain of unfair treatment from their French-speaking teachers and classmates. The same holds for Francophones who study in the English-based university systems in Cameroon (Kiwoh, 2010). The complaints of the Anglophones peaked in 2006 when it was established that for over 12 years, the Polytechnic Institute of the University of Yaoundé I had not trained up to five Anglophones. However, it became a national scandal in the same year when the then Vice-Chancellor of the University of Buea, Prof. Cornelius Lambi, allegedly recruited only English-speaking students into the first batch of the school of medicine. He was sacked for this administrative mistake.

Recently, there was a severe standoff between English-speaking lawyers and the French-speaking Attorney General of the North West Region over using French in courthouses in Anglophone Cameroon. This was only called off thanks to the negotiation skills of Barrister Nico Halle and the Minister of Justice, who called the Attorney General to order.[4]

These instances are not exhaustive. They are just some examples to show that Cameroonians have succeeded in creating a nation, but have not achieved a national official language identity and nationhood. Biloa (2012) gives further details of problems that plague the co-existence of Anglophones and Francophones in Cameroon in what he styles *"les malheurs du bilinguisme officiel."* This is because most members of the two linguistic groups view each other with mutual suspicion. This suspicion reached a point in the 1990s when some members of the Anglophone community started demanding the complete secession and independence of the English-speaking zone of Cameroon under the banner of the SCNC (Southern Cameroons National Council). These instances are a pointer to the disunity that characterises the relationship between the two official linguistic groups that co-exist in Cameroon. The situation could have been avoided if some serious reflection had been done on the kind of educational system that could project a common identity and the integrative development of the two official language groups at the time of reunification. The government at the time decided to maintain a unity in diversity with two different educational systems, which have helped strengthen the language loyalties of each linguistic group. This article insists

---

4   This information is relayed by the *Post Newspaper* No 01611 of 16th March 2015.

that the adoption of a carefully planned bilingual education system can lead to the emergence of a new Cameroonian official language identity where the citizens will not see themselves as Francophones or Anglophones but as Cameroonians with an officially bilingual identity. Such a programme should start from the nursery, primary through secondary to tertiary education. However, the question is, is bilingual education a new phenomenon in Cameroon? The section below attempts an answer.

BILINGUAL EDUCATION IN CAMEROON

Bilingual education is a phenomenon that has been around for a while in Cameroon. The government and the private sector have attempted to implement bilingual education with different aims.[5] On its part, the government creates what it calls Government Bilingual Schools, which, in effect, are two different schools operating under a principal and sharing the same campus with different vice-principals or head teachers, classrooms and teachers for the two systems of education. This contrasts with a case where the two (official) languages are used as media of instruction, as described by Hamers and Blanc (1989). This section presents what the private sector and the State have done since independence. Analyses at this point are focused on the primary and secondary school levels.

Bilingual Education at the Primary Level

The State of Cameroon has never really paid attention to this kind of education as far as primary education is concerned. Education authorities have often advocated that the government should pay more attention to the basic education sector when it comes to the dual language or bilingual education programme.[6] This makes the basis for a truly and effectively bilingual Cameroon very unsteady as children at the primary level begin developing loyalties and attitudes according to their first official languages.

However, the private sector is exploiting this void to make more revenue by introducing special schools where "one class" bilingual education programmes are practised. In this one-class bilingual education programme, each classroom

---

5 It is worth noting that many school owners use the label bilingual school as an advert. In this context, the second official language is taught as a subject
6 One of such advocates is Mr Joseph Toh Yong. At the time of making this comment, he was the Regional Pedagogic Inspector in charge of bilingualism in the Centre Regional Delegation for Basic Education. He spoke on *Cameroon Calling*, a CRTV News Programme, which was aired on Sunday, 7th February 2010, devoted to the annual celebration of the National Bilingualism day that comes up every first Friday of the month of February.

has two teachers, one English-speaking and the second French-speaking. When the French-speaking teacher is teaching, the English-speaking colleague assists in discipline while waiting for his/her turn to teach. Teaching alternates in both English and French and covers the entire curricula of the French and English educational systems as they operate in Cameroon. The time allocation is divided equally to cover the needs of both educational systems. This runs from Class One or *SIL* to Class Five of *CM1*. In Class Six or *CM2*, the pupils are separated according to the end-of-course examination they are scheduled to write. Those who choose the English sub-system of education continue with French as a subject, while those who choose the French sub-system of education only have English as a subject. The dual language or bilingual education programme ends in the fifth year because the end-of-course examinations for both education systems in the sixth year are written on the same day. Consequently, the pupils and parents have to make a choice. This kind of bilingual education, as described above, is practised in schools like Sainte Brigitte Bilingual Nursery and Primary School Up-Station, Bamenda, Horizon Bilingual Academy (HOBEC) Bonaberi, Douala, COSBIE Bilingual Nursery and Primary School Mendong, Yaoundé and New Century Bilingual Primary School Mfandena, Yaoundé (for further illustration see Kiwoh, 2010).

French-speaking pupils generally outnumber their English-speaking counterparts in all of these bilingual classrooms. The following statistics show the percentage of French and English-speaking pupils in bilingual classrooms in two schools. *Sainte Brigitte* Bilingual Primary and Nursery School Up-Station, Bamenda has 83.3% of the pupils from French-speaking background and 16.7% with an English-speaking background, while COSBIE Bilingual Primary and Nursery School Mendong, Yaoundé has 68.7% of pupils with French-speaking background and 31.3% of pupils with English-speaking background.[7] The first mentioned school is found in the heart of the English–speaking region of Cameroon, but pupils with French-speaking background make the majority. This shows some lack of interest from the English–speaking populations of Cameroon.

How the private sector handles the dual language education programme seem to pose a problem. The school operators of such institutions take the curricula of both educational systems and teach the pupils. The pupils come out over-stuffed with work, as they must learn twice what is adapted to their

---

7   These statistics were obtained from the head teachers of both schools on September 20 2014 for *Sainte Bridgitte* - Bamenda and on September 25, 2014 from COSBIE Mendong -Yaoundé.

age. This has led to complaints from their parents that the children have no time to rest or help their parents at home or play, which is essential for a child's growth. A parent, non-commissioned officer in the Cameroon Army, Chief Warrant Officer Florence Biyina, serving in Bamenda, whom we met in *Sainte Bridgitte* when she came to collect her daughter's booklist, had this to say:

> Franchement, ma fille qui est élève au Cours Elémentaire Un (CE1) n'a pas le temps de se reposer. Elle quitte la maison à sept heures pour rentrer à quinze heures trente. Aussitôt, son répétiteur doit venir pour l'aider à faire ses devoirs. Je ne peux même pas envoyer ma fille pour les courses. Même le sac d'école qu'elle porte est vraiment lourd pour son âge. Ceci parce qu'elle doit porter les livres des deux systèmes d'éducation (interviewed 20th of September 2012, Bamenda).
>
> [Frankly, my daughter who is a class five pupil does not have time to rest. She leaves the house at 7 am and comes back at 3.30 p.m. immediately; her home teacher comes to help her do assignments. I can't send my daughter on any errand. Even the school bag that she carries is really heavy for a child of her age. All these because she has to carry books for the two systems of education (Translation is mine)].

Public authorities have given a deaf ear to these complaints and have allowed school owners to continue without necessary measures aimed at regulating the syllabus adopted by privateers.

The government is making some timid promises towards implementing bilingual education at the primary school level. At the beginning of the 2010 / 2011 academic year, the Minister of Basic Education announced the creation of *ENIEG Bilingue* or Bilingual Teacher Training Colleges, to train teachers of a pure bilingual background in preparation for an eminent start of a bilingual primary education system. These institutions were located in Bafoussam, Douala, Yaoundé and Garoua.[8] However, this remains an intention, as nothing has started in this light.

Bilingual Education at the Secondary School Level

The government of the Republic of Cameroon carried out early attempts at bilingual education at the secondary education level. This was done in the

---

8   This information was broadcast by the Cameroon Radio Television (CRTV) on the 28th of August 2010 during the 8 PM news in French. The then Minister of Basic Education released this information just before Teacher Training was transferred to the Ministry of Secondary Education.

then Bilingual Grammar School Man O'War Bay, which was later transferred to Molyko, Buea. This experiment started in 1963. Candidates were selected from among the cream in West and East Cameroons and put together in one class. The method used was the "one-class model", wherein all students sat together in the same class and were taught by teachers with different linguistic backgrounds. It was done in such a way that the teacher of Mathematics taught in English while the teacher of *Mathématiques* had his or her turn in French. The students were to write the GCE Ordinary Level and BEPC certificate examinations for English and French educational systems respectively. The intention was to produce experimental batches of Cameroonians who would neither be recognised as Anglophones nor Francophones. It was hoped that this breed of Cameroonians would represent the bilingual nation's true and new identity. They were to be the flag bearers of national unity and bilingualism. The initial success of the Buea experiment led to the creation of a similar institution in Yaoundé in 1965 and then in Douala in the same year. By 1966, the first batch of students went in for the French-based BEPC with brilliant results.

However, this success was very short-lived. In 1967, all the students were to sit in for the GCE Ordinary Levels. However, to the surprise of everyone, students with French backgrounds refused to sit for the examination (Halle, 2007). Some reasons for this attitude could be advanced. The first is that English and its users at the time were considered a second class in Cameroon. Consequently, the candidates did not see any importance in writing English-based examinations. Secondly, there was the fear of embarrassment as English-based examinations were reputed to be difficult (Halle, 2007). The refusal to write English-based examinations signalled the beginning of the end of state-sponsored bilingual education at the secondary level of education. By the mid-seventies, the programme became a failure and was abandoned entirely.

During the 2009 / 2010 academic year, the Minister of Secondary Education introduced a new bilingual education programme wherein some forty selected schools were to begin teaching some subjects in English and French. Apart from the traditional subjects, Anglophones and Francophones were to study Intensive English, Citizenship Education, and Sports and Physical Education. The programme courses were to have oral and written components. The first batch of Francophones wrote what is now called *BEPC Bilingue* by June 2013, while the Anglophone candidates wrote the Bilingual GCE Ordinary Level Certificate Examination by June 2014 (www.minesec.gov.cm). However, this programme seems inadequate as no reasonable blueprint for bilingual education was presented, except for a few subjects to be taught in French and English whose impact is still to be verified.

The private sector later seized the opportunity of the government abandoning the bilingual education programme to introduce a format of their choice. Schools like Horizon Bilingual Academy (HOBEC) Bonaberi, Douala adopted a bilingual education programme where all subjects in the English and French sub-systems are studied, and the learners choose an examination at the end of four or five years. The following table shows the schedule of a bilingual class form 4 B or 3e B at HOBEC Douala:

Table 7.1 Frequency and Time Distribution per Subject in HOBEC Douala 3e B or Four B

Subject	Frequency Per Week	Total Duration Per Week
Mathematics	3 Periods	150 minutes
Mathématiques	3 Periods	150 Minutes
English Language	3 periods	150 minutes
Français	4 Periods	200 minutes
English Literature	1 Period	50 minutes
Biology	2 Periods	100 minutes
Science de Vie et de la Terre (SVT)	2 Periods	100 minutes
Chemistry	2 Periods	100 minutes
Physics	2 Periods	100 minutes
Physique-Chimie- Technologie (PCT)	2 Periods	100 minutes
Geography	2 Periods	100 minutes
Géographie	1 Period	50 minutes
History	2 Periods	100 minutes
Histoire	1 Period	50 minutes
Education à la Citoyenneté	1 Period	50 minutes
Allemand/ Espagnol	3 Periods	150 minutes
Economics*	2 Periods	100 minutes
Education Physique*	1 Period	50 minutes

* Bilingual subjects with English and French alternating

An observation of the table above shows that time for teaching is evenly distributed between the two educational systems. Out of 37 periods of fifty minutes per week, English-based subjects occupy 17 periods, representing 850 minutes (45.9%); French-based subjects 17 periods, representing 850 minutes (45.9%); and three periods for subjects that are taught in both English and French, representing 150 minutes (8.2%). Products from these institutions are usually very proficient in the country's two official languages. Some are so proficient that people wonder if they belong to one official language or the other. This experience needs to be vulgarised in an organised manner.

WHAT KIND OF BILINGUAL EDUCATION FOR CAMEROON

Cameroon has two official languages with two official language identities: the French-speaking and English–speaking identities. These two have divergent cultures in terms of education. Members of these cultures have developed deep loyalty to their educational systems. In this case, what kind of bilingual education does Cameroon need? Given the loyalty to the official languages that Cameroonians exhibit, the kind of bilingualism in Cameroon should be carefully planned. Consensus should be reached on carefully selecting what is good from each educational system and bringing the two together to make a new system. This bilingual education system should be a selection of the best characteristics of the English-based and French-based educational systems. This selection should be harmonised into a common school programme that could be used throughout the Republic, beginning with early bilingualism at the pre-primary level. We are advocating for the "one class model," wherein each teacher teaches in the language of his choice. Here, there will be no teacher for *Mathématiques* and another for Mathematics but a teacher for a subject of that nature who may decide to teach in French or English. It should avoid a situation where two educational systems run side-by-side in the classroom and move to a single bilingual education system with the aim of training Cameroonians who will have a completely new official language identity. This should run from the primary to the university levels of education. Questions that will arise are obvious: what about teacher training, books, and examination boards for such a program?

Beginning with teacher training, Cameroon's educational system is already training teachers who can function in both languages in teacher training colleges for the primary and nursery schools found in most divisional headquarters in the country. Concerning secondary education, the various higher teacher training colleges are training teachers with French and English as their first official languages. Consequently, there is just a simple need to redeploy them. This can be done such that wherever a teacher finds himself or herself, he or she can teach in the official language of his choice. This will go a long way to solve the problem where some teachers become redundant in some schools because they need help teaching in one language or another. Furthermore, a central board for the management of all official examinations would have to be created since there would no longer exist two educational systems in Cameroon but a bilingual educational system. A single examination board would replace the Baccalaureate and the GCE boards. If all these are adopted and introduced in the primary education sector, a new breed of bilingual Cameroonians will be moving into secondary school six years later. The chain will continue at the secondary and high school levels until the university. At this point, the young Cameroonians studying in this system would no longer be talking of *Anglophonism* and *Francophonism* nor having a preference for a particular language, but as bilingual Cameroonians with an official language identity that reflects the nation's bilingual character.

This sort of education can positively affect the social, economic and political lives of the polity. The impact discussed below is not exhaustive. At the social level, there shall be much cohesion in the long term. Problems arising in some public services due to communication inadequacies will gradually disappear. Cases where Francophones or Anglophones have allegedly suffered some linguistic-related humiliations in public offices (Jikong, 2003) will gradually disappear. This may not be automatic, but the gradual replacement of former monolinguals by bilinguals will go a long way to solve this problem. Furthermore, products of the "one class" education system proposed here would fit and settle anywhere in the country without worrying about language-related problems. However, individual attitudes may hinder a smooth and total integration of the two cultures.

Considering the economic impact, the gains will be both at the macro and micro levels. Today, Cameroon government spends about twice on the maintenance of the two educational systems. This increases the nation's internal debt burden, making scarce resources to be used twice for the same services that have to be provided to Anglophones and Francophones. Two schools have to be provided in areas where one could serve the purpose. In contrast, a school with a bilingual character will not only help build greater unity but will make the State spend less on providing teachers, didactic material, etc. In addition, where the means available give rise to just one school, the underprivileged group feels marginalised. An example is the lack of a secondary technical school for Anglophones in Yaoundé and other French-speaking parts and vice versa for Francophones in English-speaking parts of Cameroon. It becomes incumbent on the State to waste resources in creating new schools to satisfy both linguistic groups. However, a "one class" bilingual programme will create a new identity and a sense of belonging for most Cameroonians. At the micro level, products with this new identity will be assets to entrepreneurs, as they will play the role that two workers now play in many structures.

Politically, the impact of a new official language identity is immeasurable. The constitutional clause that states that Cameroon is a bilingual country with English and French as languages of equal status (Article 3 of the Constitution of 18th January 1996) will now find some meaning. In addition, adopting an education system that leads to the new official language identity, as proposed here, will further lead to greater national integration. The future elite that comes out as products of the "one class" system will project an identity different from today's elite.

CONCLUSION

It is true that the identity of every individual is captured in the way he or she dresses and lives, in what he or she eats and above all, in the language he uses. When English speakers find themselves in far-off French-speaking areas in Cameroon, they form solidarity groups because they share a common official language identity. This can be verified as it occurs in parts of Francophone Cameroon. The same holds for French speakers who live in the former Southern Cameroons. These linguistic groups come together because they believe they share a common identity. As proposed in this article, this could be used as a rallying force to bring Cameroonians from all walks of life to identify with each other through a new official language identity. We firmly believe that adopting a "one class model" of bilingual education will go a long way to gradually reshape loyalties and strengthen integrated development. This is in line with one of the ten points Baker (1999) proposed, which insists that bilingual education could be used to construct or deconstruct identities. Cameroon would move from an officially bilingual state to a state where all its citizens can project the bilingual identity of the nation to which they belong. If the "one class model" proposed here is adopted, officially monolingual elites will be the exception, while officially bilingual citizens, which are the exception today, will become the norm. Cameroonians' new official bilingual identity would reflect the country's bilingual nature as upheld in its constitution and reinforce the much-cherished national unity and integration fifty years after independence. However, this should not be misconstrued as the fact that a cultural definition of who is an Anglophone or Francophone has to be carefully preserved.

REFERENCES

Adger, C. T. (1998). Register Shifting with Dialect Resources in Instructional Discourse. In S. Hoyle & C. T. Adger (Eds.), *Kids Talk: Strategic Language use in Later Childhood* (pp. 151-169). Oxford University Press.

Anchimbe, E. (2005). Anglophonism and Francophonism: The Stakes of (Official) Language Identity in Cameroon. In *ALIZES, Revue Angliciste de la Reunion*, 25(26), 7-26.

Anzaldua, G. (1987). *Borderlands / La Frontera: The New Mestiza*. Aunt Lute Books.

Baker, C. (1999). *Foundations of Bilingual Education and Bilingualism*. (3rd ed.). Multilingual Matters.

Biloa, E. (2012). Le Bilinguisme Officiel au Cameroun: Facteur d'Intégration Nationale ou de Fragmentation In G. Echu and A. E. Ebongue (Eds.). *Fifty Years of Official Language Bilingualism in Cameroon (1961 – 2011) Situation, Stakes and Perspectives* (pp. 119 – 13). Harmattan.

Bucholtz, M. (1999). Why Be Normal?" Language and Identity Practices in a Community of Nerd Girls. *Language in Society*, 28(2), 203-225.

Chiatoh, B. (2006). Language, Cultural Identity and the National Question in Cameroon. In P. Mbangwana, K. Mpoche, and T. Mbuh. (Eds.). *Language, Literature and Identity* (pp. 144-152). Cuvillier Verlag.

Fordham, S.(1998). Speaking Standard English from Nine to Three: Language as Guerilla Warfare at Capital High. In S. Hoyle & C. T. Adger (Eds.). *Kids Talk: Strategic Language Use in Later Childhood* (pp. 205-216). Oxford University Press.

Hamer, J. & Blanc, M. (1989). *Bilinguality and Bilingualism*. Cambridge University Press.

Halla-Awa, M. (2007). *Bilingualism in Cameroon: Evolution and Challenges*. Gospel Press.

Jikong, S. (2003). Official Bilingualism in Cameroon: A Double-Edged Sword. *ALIZES Oracle* http://www.university reunion.fr-age of/text/74c21e88-300html.

Kiwoh, T. (2010). Official Language Bilingualism and Language Management in Cameroon. Unpublished Ph.D. Thesis, University of Yaoundé I.

Kiwoh, T. (2006). The Paradox of Official Bilingualism in Cameroon, Unpublished MA Dissertation, University of Yaoundé I

Mforteh, S. (2006). Cultural Innovations in Cameroon's Linguistic Tower of Babel. *Trans*. http.// www. internet-zeitschrift fur kulturwissenchaften 16.Nr.

Ovando C. (2003). Bilingual Education in the United States: Historical Development and Current Issues. In *Bilingual Research Journal*, 27(1) pp.1-24

Spolsky, B. (2009). *Language Management.* Cambridge University Press.

Spolsky, B. (1999). Second-Language Learning. In J. Fishman (Ed.). *Handbook of Language and Ethnic Identity* (pp. 181-192). Oxford University Press.

8

The Power of Language in Persuasion
A Lexico-semiotic Reading of Evangelisation Crusade Posters in Cameroon

JOSEPH NKWAIN

It is an atypical Thursday, 17th April 2014, morning in the Mvan neighbourhood in Yaounde. Hundreds of thousands of overwhelmed Cameroonians storm the residence of Mrs. Amougui Minkam. Jesus Christ has appeared in her spacious sitting room. As people stream in, some pass out following the eventful personal encounter, others sing praises, many meditate quietly and pray, and others present their afflictions to Him directly. As some just watch in total consternation, others make a mockery of the whole occurrence as the police (who later demand tips to allow access to the house) are called in to control the pandemonium. Public opinion is wild. The Church is alert but cautious and meticulous, as no public pronouncement is made. As the appearance gradually disappears, a sanctuary is prepared at the foot of the apparition; ecumenical services are organised with an emphasis on spontaneous donations. The steam later dies down with the final disappearance of the image. Mrs. Amougui and some 'men of God' are taken into custody and finally imprisoned at the Kondengui Central Prison on charges of defamation, falsehood and extortion. Mrs. Amougui and her cohorts had indubitably schemed up a novel, daring and dubious machination involving the peddling of spirituality for greedy intentions. Whether it was a situation of *simulacra* (mere perceptions of religious imagery in natural phenomena) or not, they had successfully persuaded millions about the authenticity of the apparition, thanks to several persuasive techniques, just like those employed in adverts and politicking. The preceding incident is very revelatory of certain fundamental aspects of human nature.

Human life is often influenced by (in)advertent choices which impact on behaviour directly or indirectly. These choices tend to measure the persuasive forces that circumscribe related contexts. As such, in one way or another, humans are consciously or unconsciously slaves to persuasion, which is why they are often persuading, being persuaded, taking decisions or making choices based on persuasion. This is reflected in the choice of food eaten, the clothes worn, drink taken, school or church attended, car or gadgets bought, life partner chosen, programs watched, etc. Life is therefore based on choices engendered by persuasion.

One tool that plays an invaluable role in persuasion is language (oral or written). As a dress of thought, the powerful influence of language over people and their behaviour has been attested in different communication acts, *viz* advertisement, politicking, commerce, evangelisation and other banal interactive situations. With regard to evangelism, the role of the persuasive power of language cannot be underestimated.

This chapter probes evangelisation posters in Cameroon, highlighting the persuasive techniques and linguistic resources employed by stakeholders in their design to lure potential crusaders and at the same time, consolidate the faith of adherents. This paper is anchored on the hypothetical premise that the power of language, especially in the domain of evangelisation, is mostly a measure of the effectiveness of the different persuasive techniques and the linguistic resources that underlie and reinforce related communicative acts.

THE NEW CHURCHES AND EVANGELISATION IN CAMEROON: AN OVERVIEW

The rise of Pentecostalism in sub-Saharan Africa has been alarming. Similarly, the proliferation of 'new churches' or 'revival churches' (as opposed to traditional Protestant, Catholic and Baptist churches) in Cameroon is no longer astounding. Expectedly, the alarming phenomenon almost parallels the legendary multi-ethnic, multiparty and plurilingual situation the country proffers. The explosion of these churches is accounted for by the following political, economic, psycho-social and religious factors.

From a political perspective, hitherto the Biya regime, Pentecostal enterprise in Cameroon was almost unheard of as it was constitutionally outlawed, and the few daring adherents were considered heretics and treated thus. This stance was reinforced by public and secret services charged with prohibiting such activities. This religious expurgation engendered the massive emigration of adherents to neighbouring countries, especially to Nigeria, where Pentecostalism had been embraced since the early 30s (Ugot and Offiong,

2013). The change of power from Ahmadou Ahidjo to Paul Biya in 1982 and the consequential amendment of the 1972 constitution in 1996 ushered in several changes at the level of religious worship as the Preamble of the constitution guaranteed freedom of religion and worship. This implied that there was no state religion, that Muslim Centres and Christian churches of various denominations co-exist harmoniously, and all observe and celebrate Muslim and Christian holidays. This constitutional amendment ushered in a new wave of influence characterised by the incursion of evangelists from neighbouring Nigeria, who found a new haven for their religious manoeuvres in Cameroon. Despite the tolerance preached, religious denominations must be officially registered to function legally. MINTAD (Ministry of Territorial Administration and Decentralisation) statistics for 2002 show that there exist only 38 officially registered churches, most of which are Christian denominations. The others are the churches that have inundated the major towns and are quickly encroaching and implanting their roots in the peripheries. As a matter of fact, the incessant establishment of bars and beer parlours, a situation which was decried at several levels, is now being corroborated by revived churches cropping up in abandoned buildings, make-shift structures, open spaces, private residents, etc. These unaffiliated denominations constitute those looked upon as 'cults' or 'sects' and are often accused of destabilising religious harmony through forceful evangelisation, noise pollution and other unorthodox activities such as extortion and deceit. Many of the denominations blame government services for slow administrative procedures and, as such, prefer to function while awaiting official recognition. The tolerance has equally favoured tele-evangelism with the proliferation of private radio and television media, which are equally supposed to be officially recognised. Today, there is a serious crackdown on these revival churches, though their resurging numbers continue to be alarming.

At the economic level, economic crises such as unemployment, salary cuts, inflation, price hikes, general unrest and the ensuing hardship have engendered ingenuity and artistry at several levels. Whereas limited resources and unpropitious taxation policies hinder entrepreneurship, religion remains a propitious haven where many find prospects. Religious practice is duty-free, and success here is guaranteed by the persuasive power of the stakeholder's tongue and the ability to lure adherents who appreciate the Lord's work in their lives and in turn, wilfully or forcibly show gratification. This, no doubt, accounts for the genuine or extorted wealth of these 'men of God.' Besides, many find in the gospel of prosperity an immediate solution to their deplorable economic situation.

The psycho-social mindset of most Cameroonians favours the upsurge of these churches. This is often pushed by the power/status situation which characterises most human societies. Psychologically, there is no feeling of attainment in so far as one's social status does not impact the vertical or horizontal relationship with interactants. Besides, the urge to play leadership roles pushes stakeholders to found or affiliate with particular denominations where they hope to meet their different aspirations.

Religiosity, in the true sense of the term, cannot be underestimated as a contributory factor. Whereas many find the Christian churches pedantic, orthodox and unfulfilling in terms of their immediate desires, they see in the new churches practicality, revival, solace and immediate fulfilment. Furthermore, the liveliness, miracles, revolutionary spirit, physical and verbal interactions often cherished during worship sessions in new churches are diametrically opposed to the solemnity in Christian contexts. Adherents therefore see in the new churches a rupture from orthodoxy to practical evangelism.

The foregoing reasons account for the proliferation of new churches and the race to win new members has been rife with ingenious strategies put in place by stakeholders. Prominent among the strategies is the organisation of evangelisation campaigns with posters carefully designed and put up in strategic positions around town. These evangelisation posters constitute the object of this investigation.

METHODOLOGY AND THEORETICAL FRAME

Data for this chapter were culled from 20 different evangelisation campaign posters put up around the town of Yaounde. This was between August 2014 and March 2015, seemingly a peak period in evangelisation activities, considering the number of posters which inundated the town.

The procedure involved taking snapshots of the posters concerned. They were later loaded into the computer for analysis, with emphasis laid on thematic concerns, spatio-temporal features, onomastics (church names), images, signs and symbols carried by the posters selected. The task constituted constructing both the probable connotative and denotative meanings embedded in the graphic signs, images and symbols on the posters while highlighting their persuasive components. Besides, the different linguistic resources exploited by poster designers were equally highlighted to demonstrate how effectively they are used to persuade potential crusaders. Posters in both English and French were exploited as almost all of them were translated for the widest readership.

However, emphasis was laid on the English texts.

This write-up adopts two approaches: the *Persuasion Model* (PM) and the *Language Expectancy Theory* (LET). The *Persuasion Model* developed by Feldman (1994) accounts for the different socio-psychological factors which engender effective persuasion. The model is represented in the diagram below:

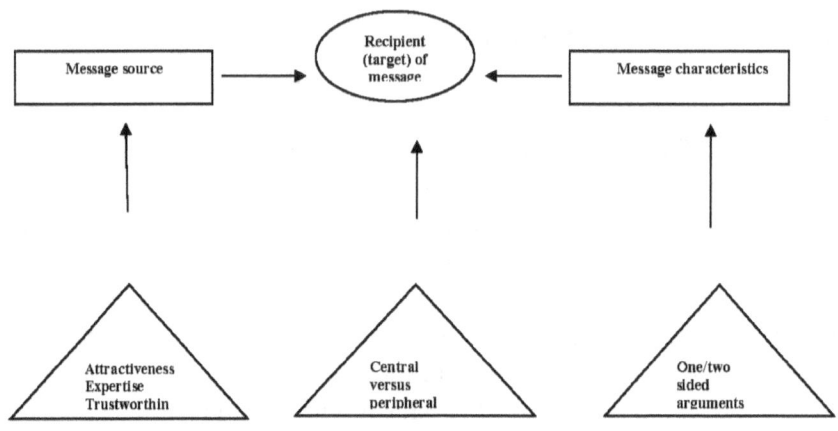

*Figure 8.1 The **Persuasion Model** developed by Feldman (1994)*

According to the model, the effective persuasive impact of a message depends very much on its source. This explains why advertisers depend so much on physically and socially attractive persons who seem to produce greater attitude change because they inspire trustworthiness and logic. Besides, a medic who argues against the consumption of bush meat (game) could be more convincing than a hunter who provides it.

With regard to the characteristics of the message, it is not only the communicator but the content of the message that affects attitude and behaviour change. Here, one-sided arguments presenting only the communicator's stance are probably best if the communicator's message is viewed favourably by the audience. Contrarily, if the audience receives two-sided messages, including both the communicator's position and the one argued against, it is probably more effective because it is seen as more precise and thoughtful.

As concerns the message recipient, the characteristics of the audience determine the acceptability of the message. The recipients' intelligence is expected to be related to their persuasability. This is because higher intelligence eases greater understanding and confidence in one's opinions such that messages with opposing viewpoints are more likely to be rejected. The model suggests that individuals of high intelligence are generally more resistant to persuasion than those of lower intelligence, though this is still subjected to verification.

The acceptability of the message is often determined by the type of information processing carried out by the recipient. This could be the central route or peripheral route processing. Whereas the former occurs when the recipient thoughtfully considers the issues and arguments directly involved in persuasion, the latter occurs when the recipient uses more easily understood information that requires less thought, such as the nature of the source or other information less central to the issues involved in the message itself. This model effectively demonstrates how authors of the messages (the evangelists beautifully portrayed in the posters) carefully choose themes drawn directly from the Bible or directly related to the individual problems or concerns of readers who use their intelligence to judge the messages and finally decide to adhere or not.

The foregoing model corroborates Burgoon and Miller's (1985) *Language Expectancy Theory* (LET), which is equally used in this paper to account for language use in evangelisation posters. The theory assumes that language use is essentially rule-based and that users often create expectations for language use and develop expected norms about appropriate language usage in given contexts. This implies that the receiver's attitude towards a message often depends on the (in)appropriateness of the message. Therefore, the appropriate or appealing message is likely to be more persuasive and *vice versa*.

Sebeok (2001, pp. 5-6), quoting Saussure, intimates that the sign is any form "made up of (1) something physical – sounds, letters, gestures, etc. – which he termed the *signifier*, and (2) of the image or concept to which the signifier refers – which he called the *signified*. He then called the relation that holds between the two *signification*. Saussure considered the connection between the signifier and signified an arbitrary one that human beings and/or societies have established at will." Sebeok (2001, p. 3) further highlights that "in human life, signs serve many functions. They allow people to recognise patterns in things; they act as predictive guides or plans for taking actions; they serve as exemplars of specific kinds of phenomena; and the list could go on and on." As such, for these signs, images and symbols to represent the values of a culture, and for them to be able to add new shades of connotation to every aspect of life and convey meaning effectively, society has to play a fundamental role in attributing and conventionalising same meaning to different signs, images and symbols. This investigation attempts to read meaning from the images, signs and symbols used and to discern their persuasive attributes.

As used in this paper, persuasion refers to the techniques used to grab attention, establish credibility and trust, stimulate desire, motivate, convince, orient, reshape, condition, inspire, deconstruct, believe, change opinion, decide, adopt, accept, etc. Semiotics handles the way signs, symbols and images are used to communicate meaning. Evangelisation is construed here as the conscious efforts of stakeholders to convince others to become Christians.

DATA PRESENTATION AND ANALYSIS

Just like in the domains of advertising in business and politicking where language is intentionally used to grab our attention, establish credibility, trust, stimulate desire, etc., language use in evangelisation posters equally exhibits similar trends with a plethora of persuasive techniques meant to lure potential crusaders to attend campaigns. Several studies attest to numerous techniques employed in different situations to convince. This section of the paper demonstrates how already identified techniques and novel ones are employed in the domain of evangelism.

Association

Association generally has to do with making implicit claims about the positive expectations of an individual with the intention of provoking strong emotional desires about specific services, ideas or products advertised or presented. In this way, these needs, likes or desires are pre-determined and associated with positive needs such as wealth, health, security, success, pleasure, etc. The emotions generated are then transferred to the situation presented in the advert, speech, etc. As such, associations such as the following are common in the Cameroonian context: *maggi cube*, a spicy ingredient used in seasoning sauces, is associated with delicious food, *omo blue*, a detergent, is often associated with perfection in washing up linen, *Samuel Eto'o Fils* (a Cameroonian football star) is associated with success, *Castel beer*, a popular brand of beer is associated with uniting people, etc. Evangelisation posters make use of the following association techniques:

Beautiful people

This involves the presentation of portraits of experts, models or celebrities who, in this case, constitute evangelists who have made a name either at the local and/or international levels. The portraits are meant to have a desirable effect on potential adherents. Generally, posters carry portraits expressive of the beauty and attractiveness of evangelists who are smartly dressed, with invigorative hairdos and attractive postures expressive of their readiness to deliver the word of God. The portraits are reflective of responsibility and verve. It is worth observing that these evangelists are setting the pace in the fashion world today as, eventually, their conspicuous hairstyles and flamboyant dress patterns are taken up by youths, especially novice evangelists.

The persuasive dimension of the portraits resides in the fact that they carry the titles and names of preachers. The titles and names play a significant role in dignifying bearers. This is clear as they often carry undertones of dignity, reverence and admiration - necessary qualities of an admirable preacher. The titles are either simple *(Reverend, Pastor, Apostle, Prophet, Prophetess, Evangelist, Brother, Sister, Wise man* and *Bishop)* or accumulated *(Reverend Pastor Tekeng, Reverend Doctor Gerald Ebile, Prophet Doctor Philip Etta, etc)*. Used simply or accumulated, the titles curry reverence and honour, thereby, revalorising the bearers.

More so, included are other attributes or positions held in church: *Prophet John Ayafor (Guest speaker), Prophet S.M. Mbote (Field 5 Superintendent), Seraphine (Gospel artist), Pastor Warah Solomon (General Overseer), Brother Mbah N. Valery (Chairman), etc.* This information further accords more integrity to the holders. Other affiliations are equally indicated: *Prophet Ticha of Divine TV, Brother Leslie N. Nsame, the African prophet, Dr Dieunedort Kamdem (Général de Dieu i.e., God's General), Mama Lydienne Tavor (Apostle elect), etc.* Apart from credibility and authenticity purposes, this is necessary referential information for traceability and attribution of responsibility.

Besides, information on the church and nationality is provided and apart from local preachers, there is a handful, especially international missionaries with affiliations abroad. For instance, *Rev. Mary Hall (USA), Bishop Leonard and Caroline Vando (USA),* etc. Understandably, a bulk of them are Nigerians such as *Pastor W.F. Kumuyi, Prophet Israel Esione* (Arena of Grace, Nigeria), *Apostle Thompson Barnabas* (Nigeria), *Apostle Paul Odola* (Nigeria), etc. Visiting evangelists constitute a novelty as they add pump, taste and variety as opposed to regular local preachers, many of whom have become household names in their various communities.

Importantly, portraits are equally indicative of marital status. For instance, *Bishop Leonard and Caroline Vando, Prophet Ticha and Pastor Schneider Ticha, Reverend and Evangelist Ambadiang, etc.,* constitute couples to be looked up to as models both in their preaching and the practice of what they preach. As couples, they incarnate and inspire responsibility.

Again, apart from titles, there are biblical first names as well as names drawn from societal virtues, *viz:* Prophet *Israel* Esione, Apostle Thompson *Barnabas*, Pastor Nji *Eclesiastis,* Prophet *Victory* and Prophet *Praise* Mbah, etc. These aspects establish an association with biblical figures and raise the expectations of adherents who eventually look up to the evangelists as models to be emulated.

Symbolism and imagery

This technique employs carefully chosen signs, images and symbols which carry sensitive messages and are meant to provoke the spiritual desires of those who immediately associate with them. To Sebeok (2001, p. 23),

> A symbol is a sign that stands for its referent in an arbitrary, conventional way ... Words in general are symbolic signs. But any signifier object, sound, figure, can be symbolic. A cross figure can stand for the concept 'Christianity; a V-sign made with the index and middle fingers can stand symbolically for the concept 'victory', *white* is a colour that can be symbolic of 'cleanliness', 'purity' or 'innocence', but *dark* of 'uncleanness', 'impurity' or 'corruption' and the list could go on and on. These symbols are all established by societal convention.

As such, some posters carry in either the fore or background, images of burning flames which could be symbolic of a *Holy Ghost* fire invoked to destroy evil spirits or an *aperçu* of hell and so, a warning to those who have not yet repented. Images of the cross, Christ carrying a cross or nailed on it are a reminder of His suffering and death for mankind, so we should be capable of such sacrifice for Him. The image of a wheelchair explicitly promises miraculous healing of the handicapped during the campaign. An image such as that with the hands of the Lord with dripping blood in the bright sky, held down towards the earth could be Christ's calling to sinners as reflected in the themes: *God is the answer, It is not late, God can still do it.* Posters carry logos used by denominations as a means of identification. Many of the logos have an open Bible, Christ's open hands, olive branches and a dove (both symbolic of peace), the globe which is indicative of the universal nature of the denomination, etc. References to contact numbers, websites, e-mail addresses are equally persuasive tools as they enable doubting Thomases to investigate, verify and ascertain the authenticity of information posted even before attending campaigns. Whereas such information is equally vital for follow-up in the case of prayers, healing, etc., the spiritual signs and symbols are meant to arouse the spiritual instincts of potential adherents.

Majority belief and group dynamics

Also referred to in the literature as bandwagon, this strategy involves capturing previous reactions, especially images of massive attendance in previous campaigns, handicapped persons standing up from their wheelchairs, etc. Such a situation is aroused by the *affiliation motive* (Morris, 1991, p. 364) heightened when people feel threatened and need that *esprit du corps* – the feeling of being part of a sympathetic group. The overflow crowd in the background insinuates that everybody has adhered and is acting accordingly and that 'you' are alone and should join others before it is late. This strategy is meant to have an inclusive effect on the reader as it urges him/her to jump onto the bandwagon since no one likes to be left behind.

Specialised jargon

This refers to the use of specific diction associated with a particular domain. Evidently, the diction here is purely religious revival diction with a proliferation of expressions such as *breakthrough, restoration, testimony, healing, prophecy, miracles, demons, demonic/spiritual attacks, kingdom of darkness, fruit of the womb, spiritual problems/wives/husbands/children,* etc. The use of this diction is meant to persuade readers that the organisers are experts, knowledgeable and aware of the predicaments of the masses. Besides, the use of this diction is intentional and meant to ignite fear which is just another effective technique.

Fear and anxiety

As indicated above, diction is strategically geared towards invoking at least one of the likely situations readers are vulnerable to. The diction is therefore meant to stoke nursed fears by exposing the vulnerable nature of readers. In addition to these expressions which appear in the section which indicates the features of the crusade, the fears are equally captured through images such as burning flames, themes such as *Expose and destroy the worries of your destiny* (everyone obviously nurses a worry), and *It's about to rain* (indicative of collective plight and necessary shelter). As the reader nurses fear and contemplates inevitable damnation, the posters provide solutions through the strategy which ensues.

Immediate solutions

After stoking fears, remedies are proposed through promises in the section enumerating features of the crusade: *healing* (with all imaginable diseases listed), *miracles, restoration, salvation, countless blessings (fruit of the womb, finances, etc.) spiritual empowerment for greatness, prophecies, breakthrough, deliverance, sanctification, etc.* Presented in a very simplistic way, these constitute immediate solutions to situations or problems directly related to the physical, psychological and socio-economic afflictions or aspirations of the people. They are thus invited for immediate solutions to their afflictions.

Evidence

This technique involves recourse to relevant information on which authenticity, reliability and credibility all depend. This presents the author as well as the information as knowledgeable, logical and reliable. Apart from the earlier described spiritual signs and symbols, authors use biblical references when themes are drawn from the Bible. These references provide the basis and relevance of their arguments. For example, *Give God no rest, Isaiah 62:6:7, Jesus is the answer, Luke 4:18, Il est l'heure de chercher Dieu (1 Chr 28:9), 'It is time to find God', A season of new things, Is. 43:19, When the winds blow, standards are lifted. Luke 4;18-19, etc.* These referrals lend intended messages credence especially as they are verifiable.

Branding

This strategy involves the strategic naming of church denominations. These names are either the same names borne by the main churches founded abroad but with branches elsewhere as denominations or are founded and christened at local levels. In any of these cases, they adopt inspiring, appealing and attractive names carefully chosen to impact 'wandering sheep'. The names tend to carry undertones of universality, divineness and grace, illumination, revival and restoration. This is one domain in which Cameroonian evangelists show their ingenuity. Names such as the following are either likely to insinuate or provoke different questions:

- *Light World Mission International* (for those who cherish to live in a world of light not darkness?)
- *Champions Faith Assembly* (for champions of the faith?)
- *Ark of God Ministries* (premonitory of another ark pending a deluge?)
- *Elohim's Family Worldwide* (direct member of God's family?)
- *The Redeemed Christian Church of God* (for the redeemed only?)
- *Deeper Life Bible Church* (deeper than which life?)

- *The Restoration Deliverance Ministries* (for restoration and deliverance only?)
- *Redemption Ground Ministry International* (for redemption?)
- *City of Glory Chapel*
- *God is Able Evangelical Mission,* and many others.

In these names, potential adherents are likely to find solace and fulfilment in their spiritual aspirations. This is with the conviction that the name of the church is reflective or representative of its activities.

Explicit claims

They constitute imperative statements which present general assertions. About campaign posters, they create reassurance, heighten the feeling of impending fulfilment and are expressed in the form of promises or gains. For example, the campaign *Takes you to three days of crossing over to 2015 without a car, Come and cross over to 2015 without carrying failure, Your life will never remain the same! etc.* The veracity of these claims is only verifiable later following 'genuine' testimonies by participants.

Bribery

As an encouragement measure, especially for those not financially viable, evangelisation campaigns are free of charge. This is usually clearly indicated on posters. This strategy is often very effective considering the impressive numbers who attend and it is thought that the situation would not be the same if participants were expected to pay to attend. This notwithstanding, participants are expected to honour their tithes (1/10th of income), requested to deep hands down their pockets during offertory processions, show gratification for God's work in their lives, and since most of these evangelists are not on regular salaries, some of them device other ingenious means to 'milk' participants.

Intensity

This technique equally heightens readers' spiritual emotions and aspirations. It presents in highly hyperbolic terms information that could have as well been presented in simplistic terms. It involves the use of exaggeration for persuasive intents. For example, a crossover night is programmed for three days as in: *Takes you to three days of crossing over to 2015 without a car.* This describes the transition from 2014 to 2015, which does not take more than a minute. *Your life will never remain the same!* insinuates total change, fulfilment and breakthrough, only, this entails a total rupture from evil ways and embracing a completely righteous life. Campaigns promise *7 days of prophetic explosions* and a *Glory and prophetic festival* instead of normal sessions of prophetic messages. In themes such as *Now is your time for an unforgettable encounter with the God of miracles, You can't afford to miss this divine encounter with the Lord* and in the promise of *a personal time with God,* physical encounters are presupposed, though this can always be questionable. Pastor W.F. Kumuyi's campaign mission to Cameroon is exaggeratedly described in terms of an impending *storm* (*Pastor W.F. Kumuyi storms Cameroon*) and is re-echoed in the theme *It's about to rain!* which is suggestive of the collective impediment of humanity as sinners. In these exaggerated terms, readers anticipate immediate remedies to their various plights.

Spatio-temporal consideration

This refers to the space and time schedules which are often as persuasive as the messages programmed. Crusades are strategically scheduled to favour time and space factors. With regard to timing, they are mostly programmed towards the end of the year from August to December and early January. This is when Christians and non-Christians alike are expected to take stock of their spiritual activities before the year runs out. This partly explicates numerous crossover campaigns during this period. This is to enable participants to start an impeccable spiritual year. Moreover, almost all the campaigns are scheduled during weekends (Fridays to Sundays) when potential participants are not tied down at job sites. Importantly, they are scheduled to begin early in the afternoon after working hours (from 5 p.m.) when many are through at job sites or with house chores. Though many consider it problematic when they turn into all-night vigils, others consider this a propitious moment to have that personal encounter with the Lord.

Concerning the place settings, they are advantageously sorted for utmost convenience. Serious campaigns are not organised in usual places of worship which are, for the most part, usually small to accommodate the masses, but in more conducive and spacious venues such as the *Multi-sports Palace* (Palais des Sports), *Yaounde, the Ahmadou Ahidjo Stadium, Yaounde, the Government Bilingual Primary School field Biyem Assi, Yaounde, the Omnisports Stadium, Douala, the Black Diamond Hall, Dragages, Yaounde, etc.* Other campaign organisers such as the Cameroon Baptist Convention blend spirituality and tourism and preferred a tourist site such as the *Lake Oku Camp Site* for their campaign of December 27 – 30, 2014. Apart from being an interesting touristic attraction, the venue favours profound meditation.

Spiritual diversion

Whereas traditional churches have been faulted for their strict orthodox practices, revival churches surmount this shortcoming through sessions characterised by interactional preaching, prophetic messages, deliverance and healing. This obtains with campaigns during which sketches, recitation of biblical verses, and above all religious music, praise songs and dance are reserved prominent places as interludes. For spiritual healing, congregational choirs, as well as renowned gospel artists, are invited to thrill participants. This was the case of *Seraphine (Gospel artist)* who thrilled participants during the crusade organised by the *Full Gospel Mission in Cameroon* from 26 – 30 December 2014. It is probable that the presence of a particular guest artist is likely to lure potential participants who often end up carried away by evangelical messages. Such sequences create a relaxing environment for spiritual communion.

LINGUISTIC RESOURCES OF EVANGELISATION POSTERS

Authors of evangelisation posters employ a plethora of linguistic devices in order to reinforce the intended message. The effective use of the devices guarantees the persuasive nature of the messages communicated. Apart from linguistic devices such as the use of *imperatives* (discussed under the technique of *Explicit claims*), *images, signs and symbols* (described under the technique of *Imagery and symbolism*), *dysphemistic expressions* (described under *Intensity*), other illuminating devices include the following:

Neologisms

Authors show their artistry through novel expressions, some of which vividly express certain religious realities. This is attested in many of the denominational names such as *Champions Faith Assembly, Ark of God Ministries, Elohim's Family Worldwide, The Redeemed Christian Church of God, Deeper Life Bible Church, City of Glory Chapel, God is Able Evangelical Mission, etc.*, described under the strategy of branding. Evidently, inspired by different spiritual convictions, the founder(s) of the denomination(s) come(s) up with names to suit their different individual or group aspirations. As earlier indicated, the denominations are strategically christened to attract adherents who find in the names personal spiritual fulfilment when/if they worship there.

In addition, there are neologisms such as *Christade* used to refer to *crusade*. In this neologism, one discerns a personal or collective commitment to Christ.

An expression such as *fruit of the womb*, often used to refer to pregnancy, has gained widespread use thanks to the rampant and preoccupying nature of the problem. Similarly, *crossover night* is now used to describe the transition from one spiritual year to the other.

Abbreviations and clipping

Expectedly, for time and space constraints, there is profuse use of abbreviations and clippings. Titles of evangelists are mostly abbreviated or clipped, *viz*: *Past.* for *Pastor, Rev.* for *Reverend, Br.* for *Brother, Proph.* for *Prophet(ess), Evan.* for *Evangelist, Dr.* for *Doctor* and *Sis.* for *Sister*. Similarly, Biblical references are equally abbreviated, for example, *1 Chr. 28:9 (Chronicles), Is. 43:19 (Isaiah)*. Again, some place names, months of the year, days and hours are abbreviated, for example: *Place: Near College ITIE (Institut) from TKC Road Junction, Aug, Sept. Oct., Nov., Dec, Jan.*, for *August, September, October, November and December* respectively. *Fri., Sat.* and *Sun.* for *Friday, Saturday* and *Sunday* and *5 PM (post meridien)*, etc. So too are some abbreviated family and surnames such as *W.F. Kumuyi, Past. Olufemi O. Lukoya, Rev. Wara L.A., Bishop Chris Raymond, Rev. Amah I., Rev. Dr. S.M. Mbote, etc*. Abbreviations and clips enable the insertion of other pertinent information in posters.

Translation

The multilingual nature of the country necessitates the linguistic process of translation, which refers to the transfer of information from a Source Language (SL) to a Target Language (TL). This is either from English to French or from French to English in this case. For a wider readership, posters carry translated versions of information featured on them. For example, denominational names, themes and features are translated: *Eglise Apostolique du Cameroun/ The Apostolic Church of Cameroon, God is Able Evangelical Mission/Mission Evangélique Dieu est Capable, Sommet Bethesda/Bethesda Summit, Divine restoration and celebration/La restoration divine et la célébration, Ta saison de restoration divine/Your season of divine restoration, Come and cross over to 2015 without carrying failure/Venez traversez en 2015 sans porter l'echec, etc*. These translations not only ease understanding, but they give potential participants an *avant goût* of the bilingual nature of the activities programmed and this constitutes an additional advantage.

Despite the invaluable role of translation in convincing participants, it is worth decrying some of the inconsistent translation versions. Evidently, either they are not done by professionals or those who do translate show some degree of incompetence or sheer negligence. This is attested in the following example where *City of Glory Hall, Obili* is rendered as *Cathédrale de la Gloire, Obili*. Not only is *Cathédrale* the unacceptable French equivalent of *City*, but the idea of a *hall* in the English text is completely eluded in the French text. The translation of the theme *Come, Jesus will give you*, as *Venir, Jesus, il vous donnez*, gives the impression of something like 'Nigerian French.' The errors of agreement inherent in the French version of *A season of new things/Une saison de nouvelle chose* (instead of *nouvelles choses*) do not only expose incompetence but should sound a note of warning to those who adventure into this domain just to come up with ridiculous translations. Though the message is effectively communicated as is often claimed, such inconsistencies put into doubt the seriousness of the entire enterprise.

Alliteration

This is a sonorous device which consists of the repetition of similar sounds in a series of words in an expression. This is used in the campaign poster by the Cameroon Baptist Convention wherein the reader is promised *Hot praises, worship, prayers, counselling and deliverance, family/group sharing, personal time with God, lifting of heart burdens, power-packed preaching and teachings*. In this stretch, *power-packed preaching* alliterates and adds to the promising vigour that will characterise the preaching. This is recurrent in the repetition of the final nasal velar /Iŋ/ sound in *preaching and teachings*. In the same text, to persuade participants, *bibles, beddings, pullovers, pens and pencils are provided*. Here, the /b/ sound alliterates in *bibles* and *beddings* just as does the /p/ sound in *pens* and *pencils* are *provided*. This device adds to the aesthetic value of the text.

Allusion

Evangelisation posters are characterised by the use of allusions attested in biblical references. For example, reference is made to most of the themes: *Give God no rest, Isaiah 62:6:7, Jesus is the answer, Luke 4:18, Il est l'heure de chercher Dieu (1 Chr 28:9), 'It is time to find God', A season of new things, Is. 43:19, When the winds blow, standards are lifted. Luke 4;18-19, etc.* In the same way, most of the features constitute acts such as deliverance, prophesying, casting away demons, healings, baptism, etc., carried out by prophets or apostles as recorded in the bible. These allusions lend credence and authenticity to promises made.

Collocation

This constitutes the strategic choice of lexical items that are loosely combined to form intelligible expressions which readers readily identify themselves with. This involves the use of appealing or positive verbal, adjectival and adverbial phrases which collocate with carefully chosen nominals. The authors make use of the following collocations: campaigns are spiced with *hot praises*, campaigns are a gathering of *champions* with *an apostolic induction* tagged *supernatural grace*, participants are promised *divine healing and restoration, salvation messages, prophetic declarations, personal encounter with God, spiritual healing, etc.* This is equally attested at the level of denominational names where churches, chapels, ministries, missions, families, etc., are tagged with or collocate with appealing expressions such as *Light* in *Light World Mission International, Glory* in *City of Glory Chapel, Champions* as in *Champions Faith Assembly*, the Redeemed as in *The Redeemed Christian Church of God, Deeper life* as in *Deeper Life Bible Church, Redemption* as in *Redemption Ground Ministry International, etc.* This persuasive lexical selection invests the texts with aesthetic value, creates symmetry and suggests credibility.

Poster authors strategically manipulate, shape and mould the foregoing linguistic resources to persuade their readers. Through the devices, one discerns the robust power of language in communicating a wide range of thoughts and in patterning behaviour.

Implication of study

Through evangelisation posters, language is once more seen as an arbitrary relationship between words and things. The arbitrary assignment of values or meaning and the mutual agreement to recognise these values are fundamental in human communication since they are essentially conventional. The posters constitute a veritable linguistic menu with a powerful influence on behaviour. Through these posters, we discern the power of language in communicating multiple shades of meaning and thought, in effecting change, in moulding reality, etc. An image, a photo, a sign or a symbol could speak a thousand words, yet, when associated with other linguistic signs, these posters exhibit a wealth of information that can be exploited for several ends. The advantage of this medium remains the fact that it combines semiotic and linguistic patterns to paint reality.

The posters constitute invested invaluable communication weapons in the hands of authors who use them not only to vividly paint reality, but to persuasively engender behaviour change. This corroborates Mbangwana (2002,

p. 18), who observes that "the symbolic power of words enables the user, the human being, to make use of both concrete and general, specific and abstract, direct and indirect, seek to persuade, stimulate emotions or remain indifferent and neutral." Like in commercial adverts wherein similar techniques are employed, readers of evangelisation posters are either influenced positively by deciding to participate in campaigns or negatively by refusing to adhere or hold res and remain indifferent. The change entailed here is determined by the different factors elaborated in Feldman's (1994) *Persuasion Model* – the message source, the message characteristics, the recipient of the message and the way the message is processed.

CONCLUSION

This write-up intended to investigate evangelisation posters in Cameroon, highlighting the persuasive techniques and linguistic resources manipulated by authors to convince readers to participate in evangelisation campaigns. The findings show that authors of posters employ a plethora of techniques ranging from association-based techniques such as beautiful people, bandwagon, symbolism and imagery. Other techniques include the use of neologisms, specialised jargon, fear and anxiety, immediate solutions, evidence, branding, explicit claims, bribery, intensity, spatio-temporal considerations and spiritual diversion. Several linguistic resources at the disposal of the authors favour the effective communication of intended messages. They include the use of neologisms, abbreviations and clipping, translation, alliterations, allusions and collocations. The study highlights that the association of semiotic and linguistic features helps paint a vivid picture of reality and, above all, plays a fundamental role in persuasion. The study also demonstrates how authors manipulate linguistic and semiotic resources to affect behaviour accordingly.

Far from developing new theories on persuasion, this paper relied much on already-established theories to demonstrate the persuasive power of language in communication. The major contribution of the paper is the fact that, unlike in previous studies wherein emphasis has been laid on persuasion in adverts and politicking, this study demonstrates how the association of semiotic and linguistic resources in a novel text category such as posters constitute an effective and powerful communication weapon. This notwithstanding, the posters could be adorned with the most beautiful images, signs and symbols, yet the fundamental question remains the necessity to verify the persuasive effect of these texts on readers. Thus, as a suggestion for further research, responses to these posters could be tracked to ascertain their persuasiveness. This could be done by sampling readers' opinions or judging from the attendance during campaigns. Besides, the response to posters could be co-related to sociological variables such as age, sex, education and status. Better still, it would be worth investigating the persuasiveness of posters in English as opposed to those in the French language, especially in a multilingual setting like Cameroon.

REFERENCES

Burgoon, M. & Miller, G.R. (1985). An Expectancy Interpretation of Language and Persuasion. In H. Giles & R. Clair (Eds.). *The Social and Psychological Contexts of Language*. Lawrence Erlbaum Associates.

Feldman, S. R. (1994). *Essentials of Understanding Psychology*. McGraw-Hill.

Mbangwana, P. N. (2002). *English Patterns of Usage and Meaning*. Yaounde University Publishing House.

Morris, G. C. (1991). *Understanding Psychology*. Prentice Hall Inc.

Sebeok, T.A. (2001). Signs: An Introduction to Semiotics. (2nd ed). University of Toronto Press.

Ugot, M.I. and Offiong, O.A. (2013). Language and Communication in the Pentecostal Churches of Nigeria: The Calabar Axis. In *Theory and Practice in Language Studies 3(1)*, 148-154.

Index

Abbreviations and clipping 138
Achebe, Chinua xvi, 1, 2, 14, 15
Adichie, Chimamanda Ngozi 1
affiliation motive 133
Ahidjo, Ahmadou 126, 136
Alliteration 139
Allusion 139
analogy 7
anarchy xvi, 3
androgyny 64, 65
Anglophone ii, xx, 87, 90, 92, 106, 107, 109, 111, 112, 113, 114, 117, 120, 121, 122
Anglophone crisis 87, 112
Antisemitism 22
apostasy 48, 69
assimilation 110
association 17, 130
authoritarianism 5

Bamenda ii, iii, xix, 111, 112, 115, 116
Bangura, Brigadier John 9
Beautiful people 130
Bible 67, 82, 129, 132, 134, 137, 140
bilingual education xix, 110, 114, 115, 116, 117, 118, 119, 121
bilingualism 111, 114, 117, 119
Biya, Paul 96, 125, 126
black 12, 13, 17, 18, 20, 23, 24, 25, 26, 27, 28, 73, 76
Black Atlantic 18
Branding 134
Bribery 135

Cameroon ii, iii, x, xviii, xix, xx, 87, 88, 90, 91, 92, 96, 99, 104, 106, 107, 108, 109, 110, 111, 112, 113, 114, 115, 116, 117, 119, 120, 121, 122, 124, 125, 126, 136, 137, 138, 139, 141, 142
Cameroon Pidgincreole xviii, xx, 87, 88, 90, 104, 106, 107
Capitalism 20
Cheney-Coker, Syl ix, xvi, 1, 2, 3, 4, 5, 6, 7, 8, 9, 10, 11, 12, 13, 14, 15
Christian 37, 42, 46, 67, 81, 126, 127, 134, 137, 140
Christianity 18, 42, 132
civil strife xvi, 2, 10, 24, 112. *See also* conflict
class xix, 3, 4, 5, 7, 10, 11, 13, 18, 21, 24, 25, 26, 46, 93, 97, 99, 100, 101, 106, 114, 116, 117, 118, 119, 120, 121
Collocation 140
colonial authority 32, 41, 44, 46
colonial cultures 110
colonial domination 34
colonialism ii, xvii, 19, 21, 30, 33, 39
colonial subjection 34
Commonwealth of Nations xvii, 30
communication 88, 120, 125, 140, 141
communicative acts xix, 125
community 16, 17, 20, 22, 34, 36, 44, 45, 48, 75, 76, 82, 104, 105, 109, 110, 112, 113
conflict i, v, ix, x, xiii, xv, xvi, xvii, xviii, xix, xxi, 1, 2, 3, 4, 9, 10, 14, 15,

16, 17, 18, 19, 20, 21, 22, 23, 24,
    26, 27, 28, 29, 35, 37, 54, 85, 87,
    88, 90, 92, 93, 94, 97, 98, 99, 100,
    101, 105, 106, 107, 108
conflict creation 100
Conflict generation language 97
corruption xvi, 2, 4, 8, 76, 94, 132
Creole iii, 3
cultural renaissance 32
cultural values xv, 52
culture ii, 3, 4, 5, 10, 18, 20, 28, 29, 49,
    77, 79, 110, 129

death 9, 10, 11, 45, 53, 58, 62, 67, 68,
    72, 73, 76, 87, 90, 99, 132
decolonisation 5, 32
Dedalus, Stephen iii, 31, 32, 34, 37, 41,
    42, 45
dehumanisation 2
deliverance 134, 135, 137, 139
development xix, 3, 4, 6, 8, 20, 22, 40,
    77, 113, 121
disease 4, 5, 10, 14, 134
dissent 14, 37
Douala xi, 110, 115, 116, 117, 118, 136
dystopian 4

ecocriticism 67, 71, 72, 78, 79
economic challenges xv
education xix, 40, 41, 42, 90, 91, 109,
    110, 112, 114, 115, 116, 117, 118,
    119, 120, 121, 142
educational systems 113, 115, 117, 119,
    120
elites 6, 121
emancipation xvii
England 36, 40
entrepreneurs 121
environment xviii, 2, 4, 32, 43, 44, 49,
    67, 68, 70, 71, 72, 73, 74, 75, 77,
    79, 80, 81, 82, 83, 94, 102, 137
Eurocentrism 3

evangelisation x, xix, 124, 125, 126,
    127, 129, 130, 135, 137, 139, 140,
    141
evangelism xix, 125, 126, 127, 130
exploitation 13, 28, 67, 93

feminist, approach 31, 54, 57, 64
folklore 32, 48
Francis of Assisi, Saint 71
Francophone 90, 92, 107, 109, 112, 113,
    114, 117, 120, 121, 122
Freetown 3, 11
French Revolution 45, 59

Garden of Eden 69
GCE Ordinary Level 117
gender 52, 64
Germany 22
Gilroy, P. 18, 28
globalisation xv
Gordimer, Nadine 1
governance xv, 5, 7, 10, 14
group dynamics 133

Haile Selassie, Emperor 18, 21, 22
hairstyles 131
hegemony 9, 35
history xvi, 1, 2, 3, 4, 7, 9, 14, 16, 19, 25,
    28, 31, 33, 34, 35, 48, 60, 71, 78
hybrid 18, 46
hybrid personality 46

iconoclasm 42
identity xv, xvii, xviii, xix, 19, 28, 29,
    30, 31, 32, 33, 34, 36, 38, 41, 43,
    46, 47, 49, 56, 109, 110, 111, 113,
    114, 117, 119, 120, 121
ideology xv, 17, 21, 22, 24, 26, 27, 34,
    37, 38

incarnation 27
individualism 13, 20, 21
injustice 19, 20, 21, 23, 25, 27, 37, 57, 93, 112
insult 89, 99
Ireland xvii, 30, 32, 33, 34, 35, 36, 39, 40, 41, 42, 43, 44, 46, 47, 48, 49, 50

jahiliyya 74
Jamaica 17, 18, 20, 22, 24, 25, 26, 28
Joyce, James ix, xvii, 30, 31, 32, 33, 34, 35, 36, 37, 38, 39, 40, 41, 43, 44, 45, 46, 47, 48, 49, 50

kleptocracy 5, 7
kola nut 11
Koran xviii, 67, 68, 69, 70, 72, 74, 75, 76, 80, 83

Lambi, Cornelius 113
language iii, xv, xvi, xviii, xix, 14, 34, 35, 39, 44, 46, 47, 60, 73, 77, 79, 87, 88, 89, 90, 91, 92, 93, 95, 97, 100, 101, 102, 103, 104, 105, 106, 109, 110, 111, 112, 113, 114, 115, 119, 120, 121, 125, 129, 130, 140, 141, 142
language merging 101, 102
Lapiro de Mbanga xviii, 88, 89, 91, 92, 93, 94, 98, 103, 104, 105
lexical adaptation 101, 103
linguistic resources xix, 125, 127, 140, 141
Literature i, ii, iii, v, xiii, 15, 50, 84, 90, 106, 107, 118, 122

marginalisation 111
marijuana 19

Marley, Bob ix, xvi, 16, 17, 18, 19, 20, 21, 22, 23, 24, 25, 26, 27, 28, 29
marriage 52, 54, 61, 63, 64, 111, 112
Marx, Karl 88, 92, 93, 101
Mbembe, A. 24, 25, 28
Mboko variety xviii, 88, 89, 101, 102, 103, 104, 105, 106. *See also* Lapiro de Mbanga
Mda, Zakes 1
Mecca 70, 73, 76, 81, 82
mediation xv, 40
methodology 94
missionaries 131
modernism xvii, 30, 34, 46, 47
Mongo Beti 1
mother tongue 88, 89
Mozambique 22, 41
music ii, xvi, xviii, 16, 17, 18, 19, 20, 21, 22, 24, 25, 27, 28, 60, 87, 90, 91, 92, 96, 102, 105, 137
 musicians 18, 88, 91, 92, 94, 105
Muslims 68, 70, 72, 73, 74, 75, 77, 80. *See also* Christians
mythology 6, 37, 78, 79, 81

national integration 121
nationalism 32, 33, 34, 36, 44, 45, 46, 49
nationalist agenda xvii, 30, 39
national unity xix, 110, 111, 117, 121
Neologisms 137
Ngugi, wa Thiongo xvi, 1, 2, 15, 17
Nigeria 125, 126, 131, 142
noise pollution 126

Osundare, Niyi 1

paradise xviii, 36, 67, 68, 69, 71, 72, 73, 76, 77, 80, 82, 83
paternity 31
patronage networks 8
peasants 11, 12, 13, 76

pedagogy 37, 41, 43
Pentecostalism 125
Persuasion Model xi, 128, 141
phallocracy 52, 56
poetry ii, xvi, 1, 2, 3, 4, 7, 9, 12, 13, 14, 42, 52, 53, 56, 60, 61
politics xvi, 2, 3, 4, 6, 8, 17, 24, 29, 32, 33, 39, 40, 43, 49
postcolony xvi, 2, 24, 27, 28
post-independence 2, 3, 5, 6, 7, 8, 10, 14, 17, 18, 19, 25
Poverty 4
power xvi, xix, 2, 5, 6, 7, 8, 9, 10, 11, 13, 14, 24, 52, 78, 92, 93, 94, 99, 101, 112, 125, 126, 127, 139, 140, 141
prophecy 14, 133
psychic energy 54

race 16, 20, 21, 22, 23, 24, 28, 29, 34, 46, 49, 67, 73, 79, 127
racism 21, 22, 23, 24, 29
Rastafarian 18, 19. *See also* Reggae
rationalisation 32, 34, 40
Reggae 18, 19, 27
religion xv, 18, 19, 33, 37, 39, 40, 67, 77, 126
  Islam xviii, 19, 68, 74, 75, 77, 83
reunification 111, 113
revolution 4, 13, 25
ritual 19, 34, 37, 70, 83
Roman Catholicism 37
Rushdie, Salman ix, xvii, 67, 68, 69, 70, 71, 72, 74, 75, 76, 77, 78, 80, 81, 82, 83, 84

Saussure 129
sexual harassment 59
Sierra Leone ix, xvi, 1, 2, 3, 4, 5, 6, 7, 8, 9, 10, 11, 13, 14, 15
slavery 3, 25
Social Conflict Theory xviii, 88, 92
social justice 8

solidarity groups 121
South Africa 15, 22, 24
Soyinka, Wole 1
spear words 87, 88, 89, 94, 96, 100
Spiritual diversion 137
spiritual healing 137, 140
spirituality 19, 72, 73, 80, 81, 82, 124, 136. *See also* religion
suffering 10, 11, 12, 13, 14, 24, 61, 132
suicide 11, 75
symbolism 13, 44, 76, 132, 137, 141

terrorism 17
theory ii, iii, xvii, 2, 23, 64, 67, 79, 92, 93, 99, 101, 105, 129
traumatic sites 1
tribalism 8
Trump, Donald J. 23

unemployment 97, 126
United Kingdom xvii, 30
United States vi, 22, 23, 24, 109, 123

violence xv, 3, 7, 13, 14, 20, 22, 24, 26, 27, 48

war xvi, xvii, 1, 2, 3, 4, 5, 7, 10, 13, 14, 21, 22, 23, 27, 32, 55, 64. *See also* conflict
white supremacist cults 23
Woolf, Virginia ii, ix, xvii, 32, 49, 50, 51, 52, 53, 57, 58, 59, 60, 61, 62, 63, 64, 65, 66

www.ingramcontent.com/pod-product-compliance
Lightning Source LLC
Chambersburg PA
CBHW032005220426
43664CB00005B/147